For all portable keyboards *by Kenneth Baker.*

THE COMPLETE KEYBOARD PLAYER

OMNIBUS EDITION

Welcome to the fascinating world of
home music-making.

This course has been written to
help you get the best out of your
electronic keyboard. It will be of great
use to teachers, both private and classroom.

BOOK 1

Two important features of Book One are
the pull-out chord chart, and the record,
on which the author plays selected songs and
exercises from Book One.

Exclusive Distributors:
Music Sales Limited
8/9 Frith Street, London, W1V 5TZ, England
Music Sales Pty. Limited
120 Rothschild Avenue, Rosebery, NSW 2018, Australia

This book © Copyright 1984 by
Wise Publications
ISBN 0.7119.0748.X
Order No. AM 60476

Music Sales complete catalogue lists thousands of
titles and is free from your local music book shop,
or direct from Music Sales Limited.
Please send £1.00 in stamps for postage to
Music Sales Limited, 8/9 Frith Street, London, W1V 5TZ.

Printed and bound in Great Britain by
Anchor Press Ltd., Tiptree, Essex.

Wise Publications
London/New York/Sydney/Cologne

BOOK 1

BOOK 2

BOOK 3

LAYOUT OF THE KEYBOARD

1 Your electronic keyboard looks
something like this:—

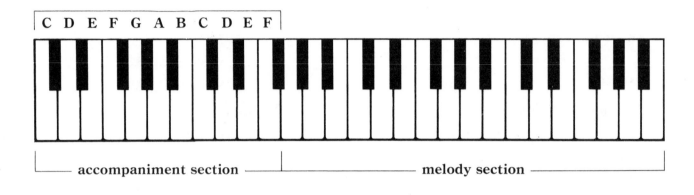

The left hand section of the keyboard is
used for the **accompaniment.** Just
playing single notes here can give you a
truly professional-sounding background to
your songs.

The remainder of the keyboard is used
for the **melody.**

BLACK KEYS

2 The black keys are grouped like this:—

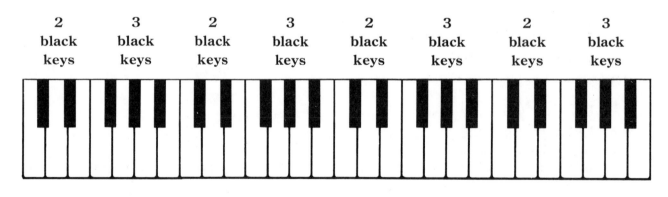

You need these black key groups in order
to locate the white keys.

NAMES OF THE NOTES

3 Punch out the cardboard "keyboard guide" which comes with this book. Select the one that fits, or most nearly fits your keyboard, and place it behind the keys.

You will see from the guide that there are only seven different letter names:

A B C D E F G

These keep repeating throughout the keyboard.

NOTE C

4 Let's learn "C" first.

Pick out all the C's from the guide (there will be three, four or five of them, depending on your keyboard model). Note that these C's lie directly to the left of each of the groups of two black keys:—

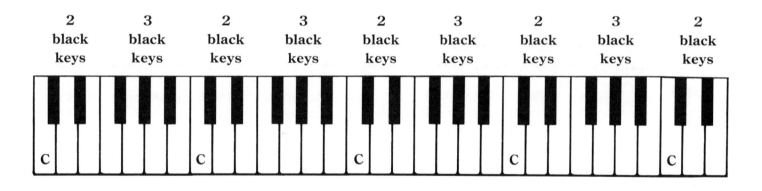

| 2 black keys | 3 black keys | 2 black keys | 3 black keys | 2 black keys | 3 black keys | 2 black keys | 3 black keys | 2 black keys |

Remove your guide from the keys for a moment and locate all the C's without its help.

THE OTHER SIX NOTES

5 Use the black note groupings to locate **D, E, F, G, A,** and finally **B.** Check with your keyboard guide to begin with, then try locating the notes without the guide.

Spend a little time each day "note finding", and before you know it, you will be able to dispense with your keyboard guide altogether — which means, of course, that you can concentrate more on the **music.**

SINGLE-FINGER CHORDS

Now let's start to play.

Switch on your keyboard and select "single-finger chords" (refer to your owner's manual for the position of this function).

In the "accompaniment" section of your keyboard, play the note C with the index finger of your left hand. If you have a choice of two C's, play the upper one, i.e. the one to the right:—

C

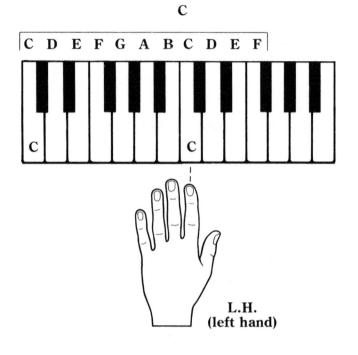

L.H.
(left hand)

You are hearing a chord of "C" (three notes playing together).

FINGERED CHORDS

This is an alternative, and far more productive way of using your left hand. I advise you to adopt it right from the start.

Switch on your keyboard and select

"fingered chords" (refer to your owner's manual).

In the "accompaniment" section of your keyboard, play the following three notes together:—

C

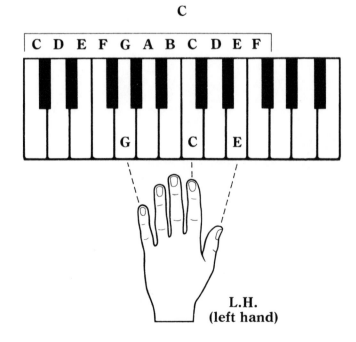

L.H.
(left hand)

This time you are hearing, and actually playing, a chord of C.

RHYTHM

Now let's add rhythm to your chord of C.

In the section of your instrument marked "rhythm", select "Rock". Press the start button and a rock-style drum rhythm will begin. Set the "tempo" (speed) button control to "medium".

Play and hold the note C (if using the "single-finger chord" method), or play and hold the complete C chord (if using the "fingered chord" method). You will hear an accompaniment, consisting of:—

bass note(s)

chord of C

drums

MEMORY

If you have a "memory" button press it now. This will "lock" the C chord into the memory, and you may remove your left hand from the keyboard altogether.

Try other rhythm patterns, such as "Swing", "Waltz", "Bossa Nova", and so on. Leave the memory button on, and the keyboard will continue to play on its own.

When you have finished experimenting with the rhythms come back to "Rock", and stop the rhythm.

FINGER NUMBERS

10 Your fingers are numbered from 1 to 5, like this:—

L.H.
(left hand)

R.H.
(right hand)

- Your left hand plays the accompaniment.

- Your right hand plays the melody.

G CHORD

11 In order to play the accompaniment to your first song, *Merrily We Roll Along,* you need to learn a new chord: G.

Using single-finger chord method:

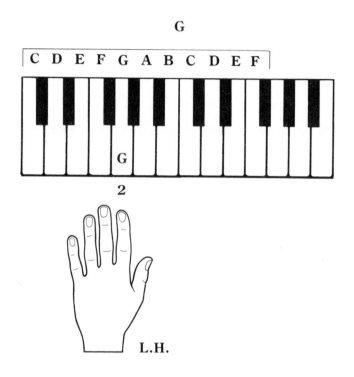

Using fingered chord method:

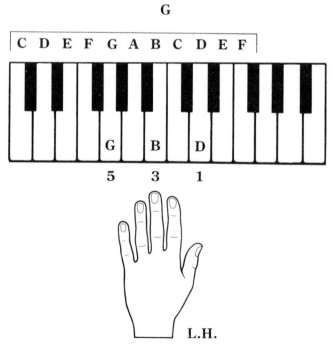

Before going any further, check your keyboard settings:—

Single-finger chords, or fingered chords + Memory (if available).

Rhythm: rock

Tempo: medium

PLAYING C AND G CHORDS, WITH RHYTHM

12 Press the rhythm "start" button with your right hand exactly as your left hand plays the "C" Chord. The accompaniment will begin.

Alternatively, press the "synchro-start" button (if you have one). The accompaniment will begin as soon as your left hand strikes the first note(s).

Let the C Chord and its rhythm play for a while, then change to the G Chord.

After a while change back to C.

NOTES ON CHORD CHANGING

13 When using the single-finger chord method:

● Play only one note at a time. Never let notes overlap.

When using the fingered chord method, without "memory":

● If the chords being changed have a note in common, don't bother to re-strike that note. e.g.:

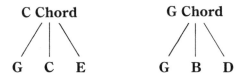

● The note G is common to both chords, so hold it down throughout any chord changing.

When using either chord method:

● If you have a flashing "tempo" light*, try to change your chords on a flash (more of this later).

* refer to your owner's manual.

USING THE RECORD

14 Now listen to band 1 (the accompaniment to "Merrily We Roll Along") of the record included with this book. The written music for this appears below. Follow the music through as you listen to the record.

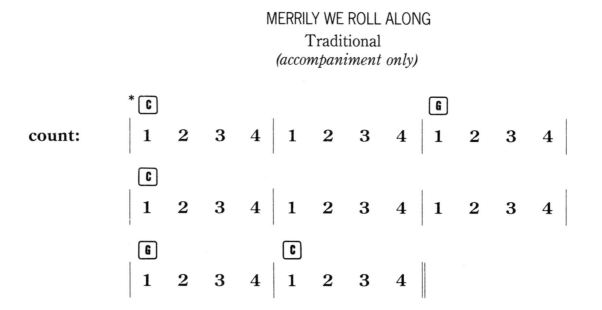

MERRILY WE ROLL ALONG
Traditional
(accompaniment only)

Notice how my counting on the record fits in naturally with the rhythm of the drums. Notice also that the counting tells you where to change chords.

Listen to the record again and play your chords along with it. Note: Don't press your "rhythm start" button this time. This is because it is virtually impossible to synchronise the rhythm sections of two keyboard instruments, so use only the rhythm section on the record.

How did you get on? Are you changing your chords cleanly and at the right time?. . . .

Play the piece on your own now, using your own rhythm accompaniment.

* If you do not have a "memory" function on your keyboard, hold each chord down until the next chord symbol appears.

ACCENTS AND BAR LINES

15 While you were playing, did you feel a
natural accent occurring on every count
"1"?

$$\underline{1} \quad 2 \quad 3 \quad 4 \quad , \quad \underline{1} \quad 2 \quad 3 \quad 4 \quad \text{(etc.)}$$

If you have a tempo light, this is where it
is designed to flash: on every count 1.

Play again and check this out.

If you look again at the music to *Merrily
We Roll Along*, you will see that a series
of vertical lines, called "bar lines", have
been drawn in front of every count 1:—

MERRILY WE ROLL ALONG

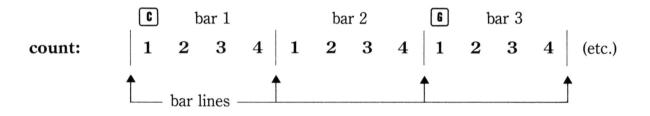

As well as indicating the position of the
natural accents, bar lines divide the music
up into "bars", or "measures". So every
song has a bar 1, a bar 2, and so on.

WALTZ: BARCAROLLE

16

In "Merrily We Roll Along" there were 4 beats (counts) to the bar.

In your next song, *Barcarolle*, the natural accents occur every 3 beats (counts). Barcarolle can therefore be said to have "3 beats in a bar". Such a song is called a "Waltz".

Before you play *Barcarolle*, set your keyboard as follows:—

Single-finger chords, or fingered chords, + Memory (if available).

Rhythm: waltz

Tempo: medium.

Listen to the record first (band 2), to get the feel of the song, then play along with the following (chords only, no rhythm):—

BARCAROLLE
Offenbach

count:

|C| 1 2 3 | 1 2 3 | |G| 1 2 3 | 1 2 3 |

| 1 2 3 | 1 2 3 | |C| 1 2 3 | 1 2 3 |

| 1 2 3 | 1 2 3 | |G| 1 2 3 | 1 2 3 |

| 1 2 3 | 1 2 3 | |C| 1 2 3 | 1 2 3 |

How did you get on, following the record?. . . .

All right, press your rhythm "start" button now and play the piece on your own. Don't forget to count the beats.

PLAYING THE MELODY: MIDDLE C

17 Now let's learn how to play melodies, so that you can play the complete versions of *Merrily We Roll Along*, and *Barcarolle*.

Look again at your "keyboard guide" and you will see that one of the C's is circled. This C, which lies roughly in the middle of the instrument, is called Middle C:—

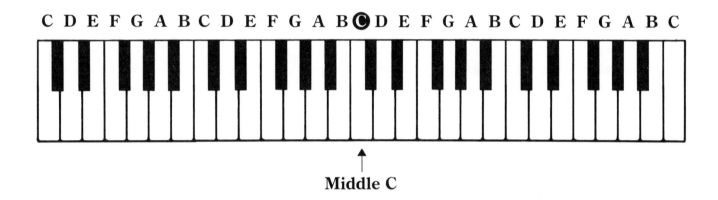

Middle C

Most of your first melody playing will take place around Middle C.

Place your right thumb (finger number 1) on Middle C and cover the next four adjacent notes with the tips of your remaining four fingers:—

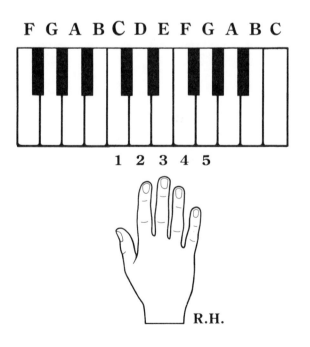

R.H.

The notes covered in the above diagram are:

MIDDLE C, D, E, F, G

THE WRITTEN MUSIC

18

This is how these five notes are written down in music:—

Treble clef (used for right hand notes)

Notice how two of the notes (E, G) appear on lines, two of the notes (D, F) appear in spaces, and one of the notes (Middle C) has its own little line (called a "ledger" line).

TIMING

19

The stave (the group of five long lines, shown above) determines the "pitch" of the notes. It tells you whether the note is C, D, E, etc. But you need to know also how long each note is to last. This aspect of music, called "timing", is written like this:—

time note	name	lasting
♩ or	quarter note (crotchet)	1 beat (or count)
♩ or	half note (minim)	2 beats (or counts)
♩. or	dotted half note (dotted minim)	3 beats (or counts)
o	whole note (semibreve)	4 beats (or counts)

Here are some examples of written notes,
showing both "pitch" and "time":—

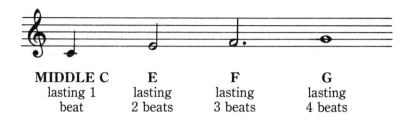

MIDDLE C	**E**	**F**	**G**
lasting 1 beat	lasting 2 beats	lasting 3 beats	lasting 4 beats

REGISTRATION

20

You are almost ready now to play the melody of "Merrily We Roll Along".

First you must set up the right hand (melody) section of your keyboard:—

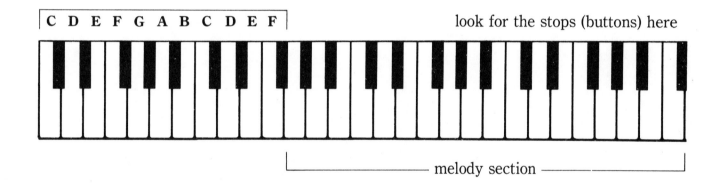

look for the stops (buttons) here

————— melody section —————

There are many different sounds available in your melody section★. There are orchestral sounds, such as flute, trumpet, and violin; percussive sounds such as piano, harpsichord, and vibes; and "odd" sounds such as synthe, fantasy, funny, and so on. Feel free to experiment with these different effects and don't be afraid to change your mind each time you play.

Sound set ups are called "registrations", and I will be giving "suggested registrations" for each piece, which you may, or may not, wish to follow.

★ refer to your owner's manual for details.

MERRILY WE ROLL ALONG

Traditional

Suggested registration: *piano*

Rhythm: rock
Tempo: medium (♩ = 88)*

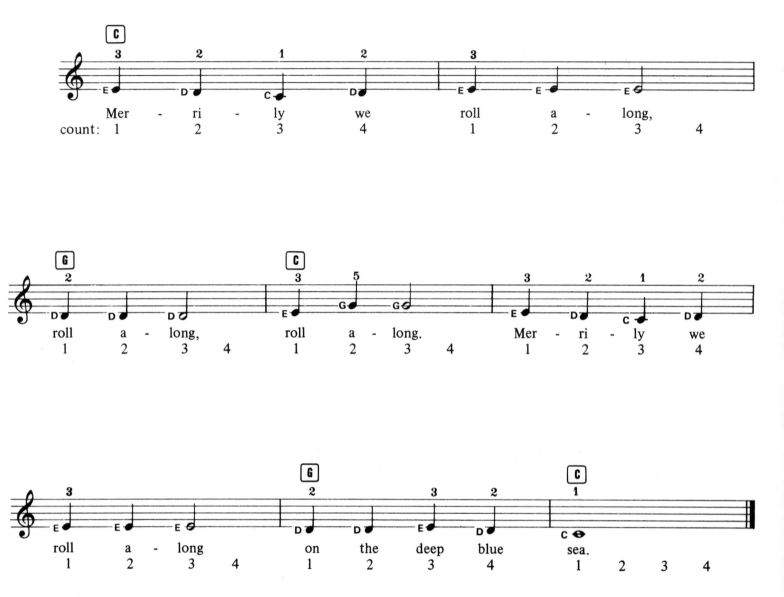

* Metronome marking. A metronome is
an instrument which indicates the speed
of a piece of music. Although not
absolutely necessary, you may buy one if
you wish at your local music dealer.

SUGGESTED PRACTICE ROUTINE FOR "MERRILY WE ROLL ALONG"

21

1. Listen to *Merrily We Roll Along* on the record (band 3), following the written music through as you do so.

2. Play the melody on its own with your right hand. You begin on note "E" with your 3rd finger.

3. When you are reasonably fluent with the notes, start to count the beats (1, 2, 3, 4, and so on). At this stage it may help if you add "drums" (no left hand chords). Start playing your melody WITH the tempo light; it flashes every four beats with this Rock rhythm.

4. Play your melody along with the record.

5. Revise the accompaniment. Play the accompaniment through (left hand only), counting 1, 2, 3, 4, etc. Check your accompaniment against the record if necessary.

6. Play accompaniment only and hum the melody through with it. This is an important stage. Try and imagine playing the melody notes as you do this.

7. Play melody and accompaniment together. Note: To help you get started, let the accompaniment run for a few bars on Chord C before coming in with the melody. Always start your melody on a tempo light.

8. If you wish, you may now play your complete *Merrily We Roll Along* with the record, **but do not press your "rhythm start" button.**

TIME SIGNATURE

22

Now let's play *Barcarolle*.

This song, you will remember, has three beats to the bar. These beats are quarter notes (crotchets): ♩ ♩ ♩

This is indicated at the beginning of the piece, like this:— **3/4**

meaning: three 'quarter notes' to the bar.

This is called: the Time Signature.

BARCAROLLE
(FROM "THE TALES OF HOFFMAN")
By Jacques Offenbach

Suggested registration: horn, or trumpet

Rhythm: Waltz
Tempo: medium (♩ = 88)

TIME SIGNATURE

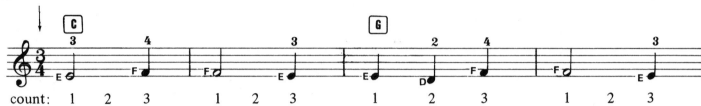

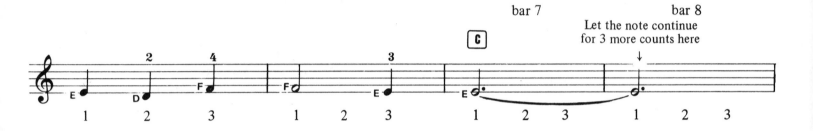

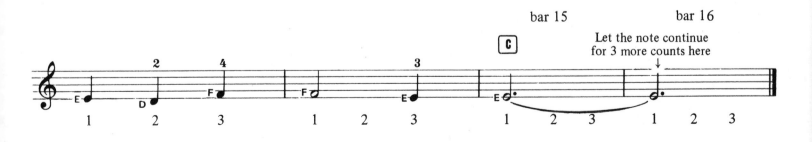

SUGGESTED PRACTICE ROUTINE FOR "BARCAROLLE"

23

1. Listen to "Barcarolle" on the record (band 4), following it through with the written music.

2. Play the melody on its own. Count the timing (1, 2, 3, etc.)

3. Play the melody along with the record.

4. Revise the accompaniment.

5. Play the accompaniment and hum the melody through with it.

6. Play melody and accompaniment together.

TIES

24

Each of the time notes:—

		lasting
♩	quarter note (crotchet)	1 beat
♩	half note (minim)	2 beats
♩.	dotted half note (dotted minim)	3 beats
o	whole note (semibreve)	4 beats

may be extended by the use of a TIE. A tie is a curved line connecting two notes of the same pitch:—

Barcarolle (bars 7 and 8, and bars 15 and 16)

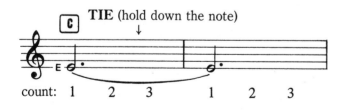

Here you play the first E and count for the second E also without striking the note again. Total time: 6 beats.

Look out for more ties in the songs which follow.

Work out your own "practice routine" for the new songs, using the record as before.

LIGHTLY ROW

Traditional

Suggested registration: trumpet

Rhythm: swing
Tempo: medium (♩ = 92)

WHITE ROSE OF ATHENS

Music by Manos Hadjidakis
Words by Norman Newell
Additional Words by Archie Bleyer

Suggested registration: clarinet
+ arpeggio (if available)

Rhythm: rhumba
Tempo: fairly slow (♩ = 84)

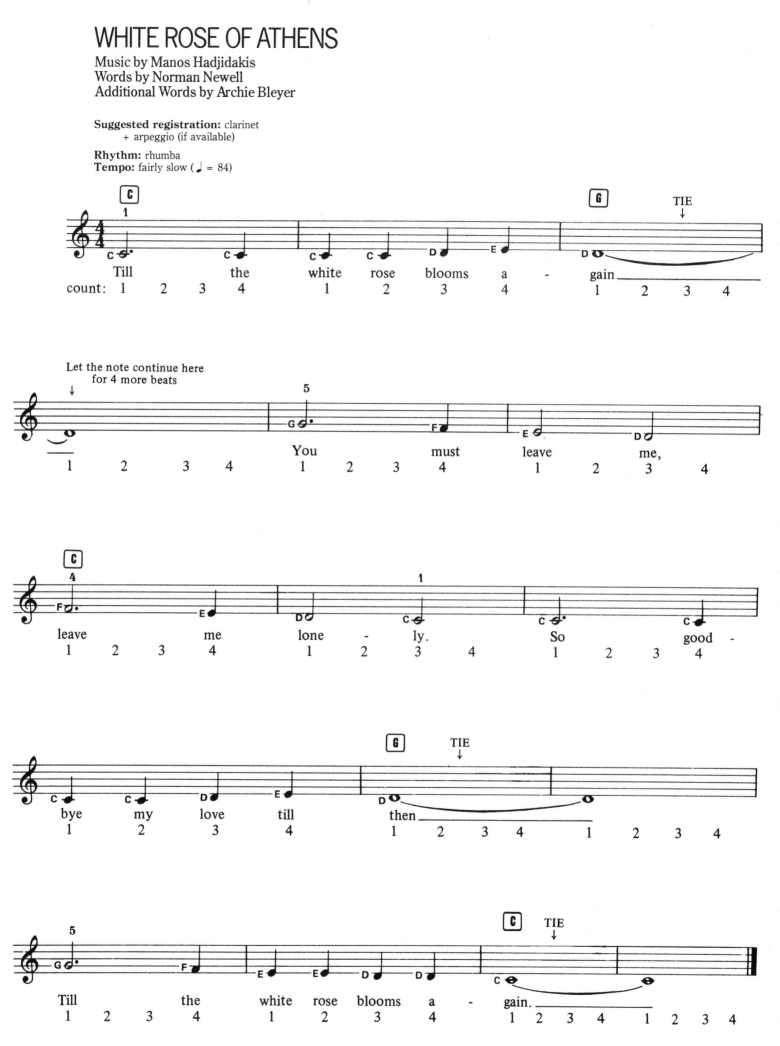

NEW CHORD: F

25 Using single-finger chord method:

F

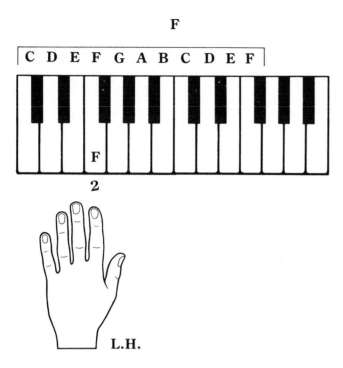

Using fingered chord method:

F

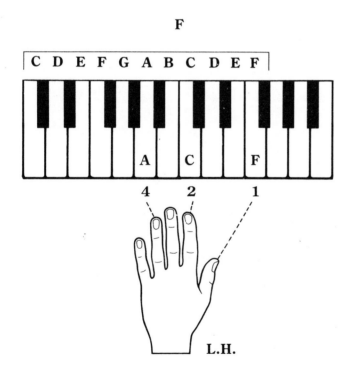

PICK-UP NOTES

26 Songs do not always begin on beat 1. In your next song: *Banks Of The Ohio,* the melody has three notes before the first beat 1. These preliminary notes are called "pick-up notes":—

BANKS OF THE OHIO, p. 24

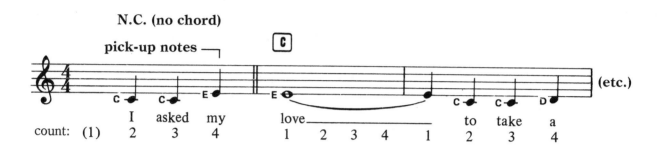

Beats missing from the pick-up bar appear (usually) in the last bar of the song:—

BANKS OF THE OHIO

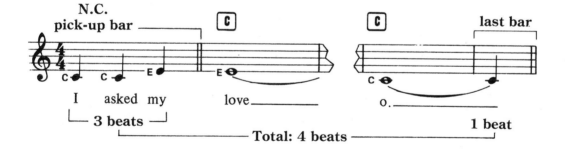

Note: It is usual to play "no chord", written: "N.C.", during pick-up notes.

BANKS OF THE OHIO

Traditional

Suggested registration: flute

Rhythm. rhumba, or beguine
Tempo: medium (♩ = 100)
Synchro-start, if available

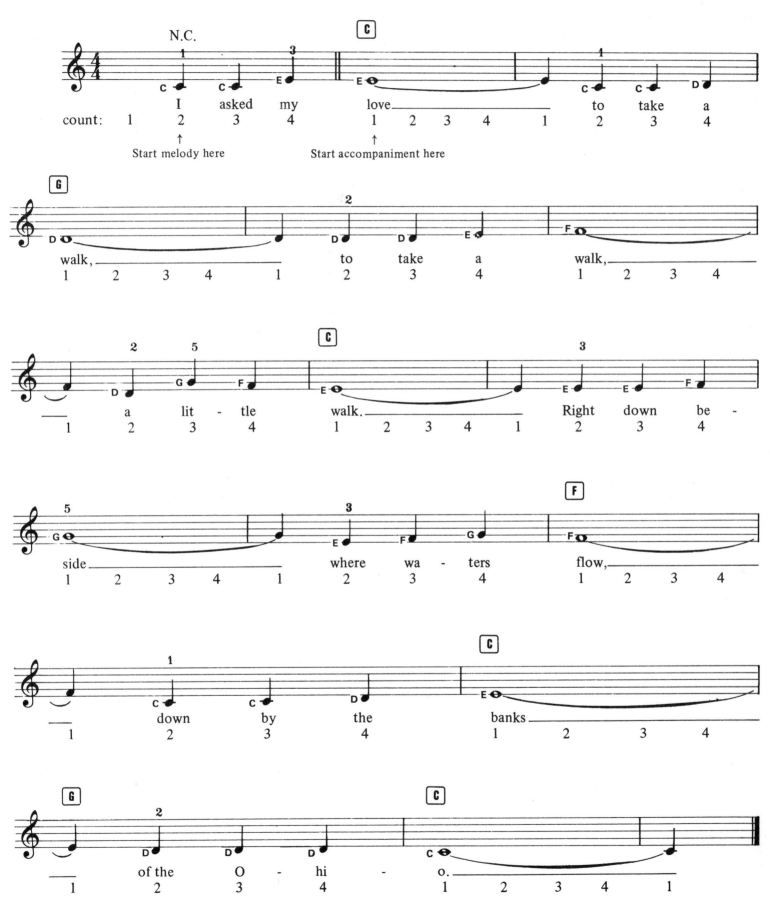

WHEN THE SAINTS GO MARCHING IN

Traditional

Suggested registration: trumpet

Rhythm: swing
Tempo: moderately fast (♩ = 138)
Synchro-start, if available

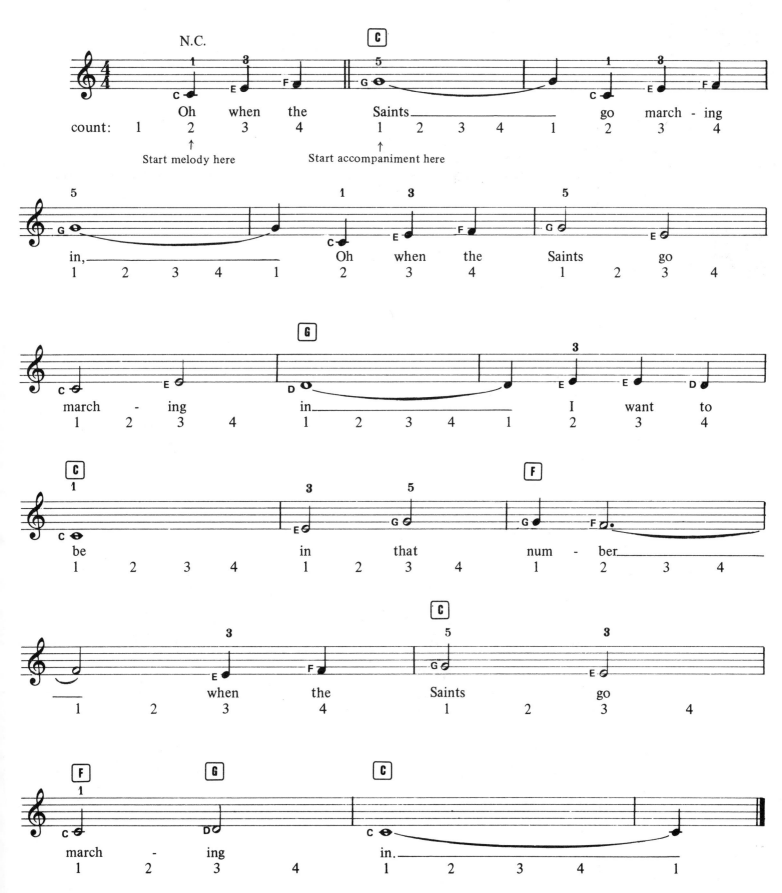

THREE NEW NOTES: A, B, C, FOR RIGHT HAND

27

FINGERING NEW NOTES

28 When any new notes appear extend your hand to play them. Allow your hand to return to its normal relaxed position (one finger per note) as soon as possible:—

LARGO, p. 28

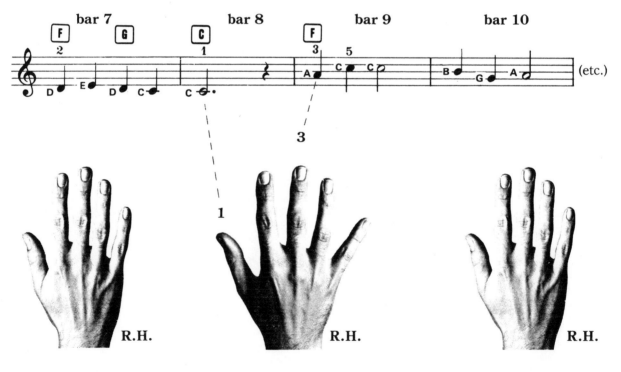

normal hand position
(covering C, D, E, F, G)

extend hand

normal hand position
(now covering F, G, A, B, C)

Follow the written fingering and you can't go wrong.

RESTS

Silences are often called for in music. In order to indicate these, symbols called "rests" are used. Each of the Time Notes has its own rest:—

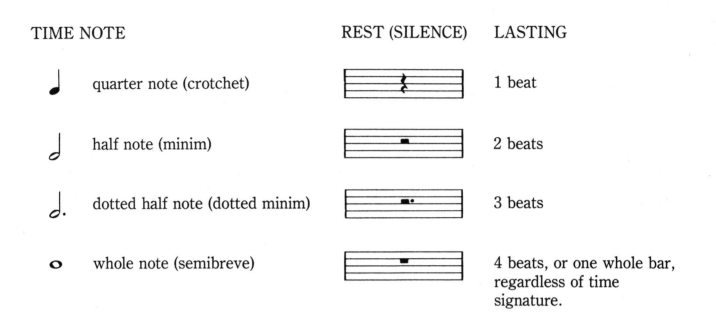

TIME NOTE		REST (SILENCE)	LASTING
♩	quarter note (crotchet)		1 beat
♩	half note (minim)		2 beats
♩.	dotted half note (dotted minim)		3 beats
o	whole note (semibreve)		4 beats, or one whole bar, regardless of time signature.

Rests are used mainly for musical or dramatic reasons. However, they are often useful for moving your hand from one part of the keyboard to another:—

LARGO, p. 28

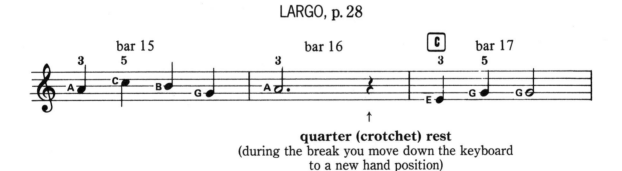

quarter (crotchet) rest
(during the break you move down the keyboard
to a new hand position)

LARGO
("FROM THE NEW WORLD")
By Antonin Dvořák

Suggested registration: oboe

Rhythm: bossa nova
Tempo: slow ($\rlap{/}{\downarrow} = 80$)

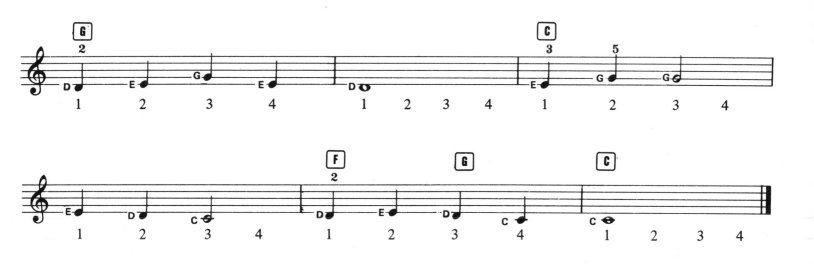

MICHAEL ROW THE BOAT ASHORE

Traditional

Suggested registration: *jazz organ*
  + tremolo

Rhythm: rock
Tempo: medium (♩ = 100)
Synchro-start, if available

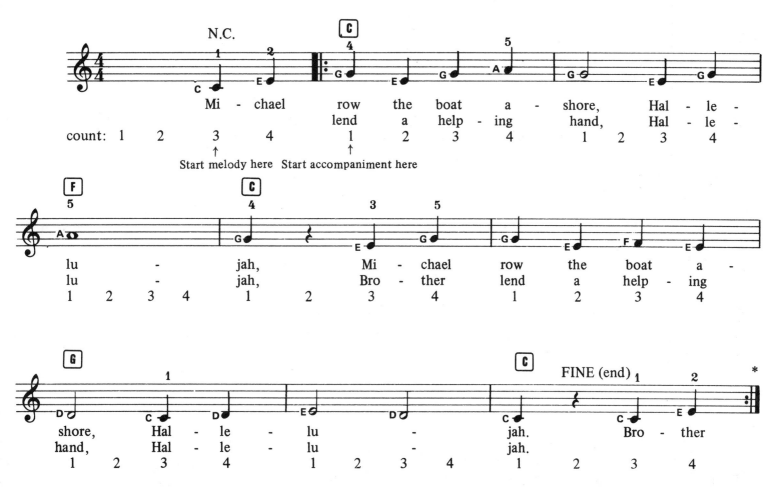

* Repeat Mark. Go back to the matching
sign ‖: and play through again until
"FINE": the end of the piece.

WOODEN HEART

Words & Music by Fred Wise, Ben Weisman, Kay
Twomey & Berthold Kaempfert

Suggested registration: piano

Rhythm: swing
Tempo: moderately fast (♩ = 144)
Synchro-start, if available

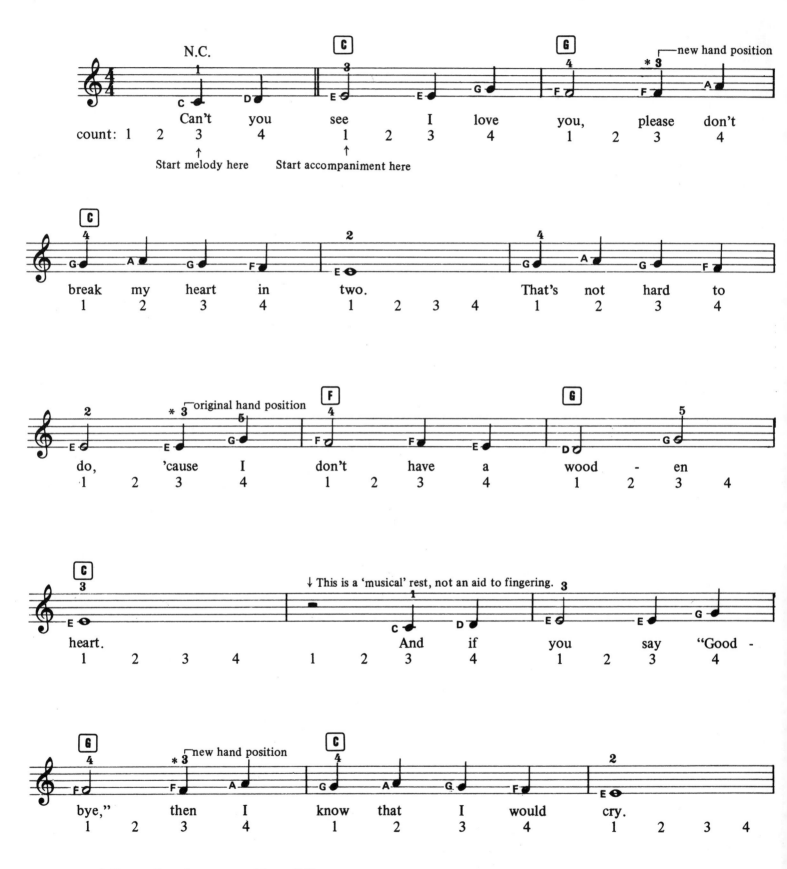

* Re-strike the note with a different
finger, as shown.

THIS OLE HOUSE

Words & Music by Stuart Hamblen

Suggested registration: saxophone

Rhythm: swing
Tempo: fast (♩ = 208)
Synchro-start, if available

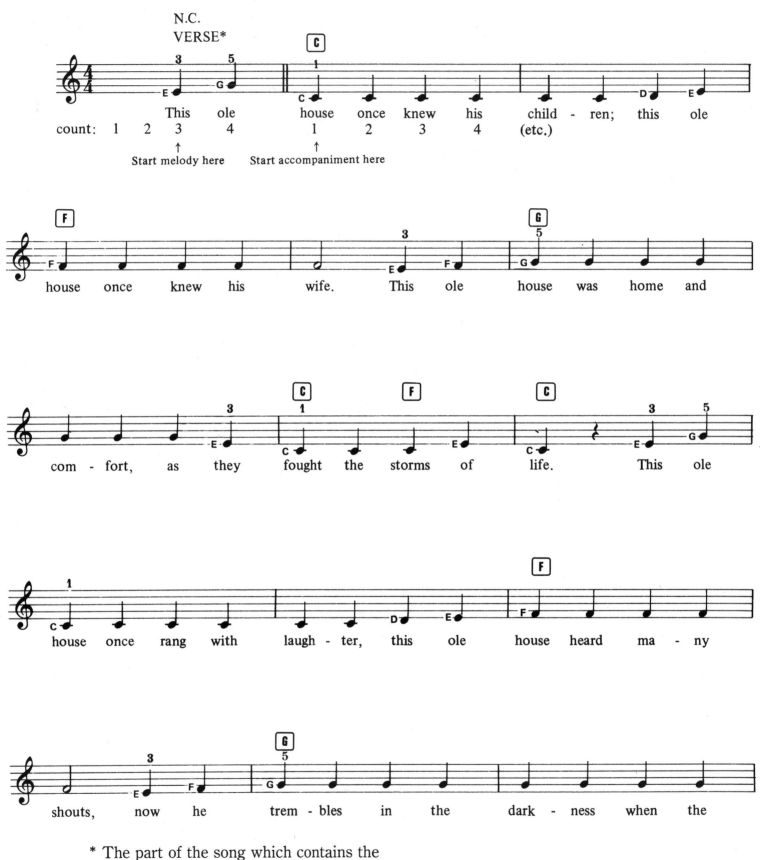

* The part of the song which contains the
bulk of the narrative. Usually sung by a
solo singer.

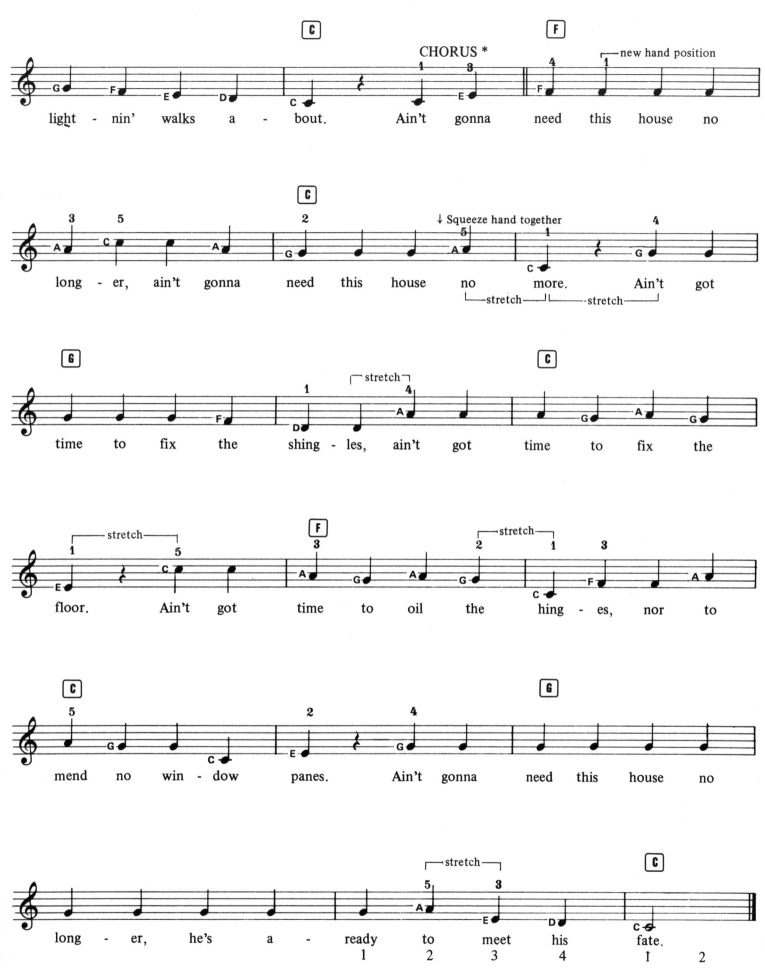

EIGHTH NOTES (QUAVERS)

The eighth note, or quaver, is another sort of time note:—

eighth notes (quavers)

Eighth notes move twice as fast as your basic quarter note (crotchet) beat:—

So each eighth note is worth half a beat.

If you say the word "and" in between your beat numbers you will get the feel of the eighth note:—

eighth note example:

count: 1   2   3   4   1 and 2 and 3 and 4 and

Listen to this example on the record (band 10). Notice how I keep the speed of my basic beats the same throughout.

Like the other time notes, the eighth note has its own rest—

eighth (quaver) rest	equivalent to	lasting
𝄾	♪	½ (quarter note) beat

Count eighth rests in exactly the same way that you would count eighth notes:—

SUPER TROUPER, p. 36

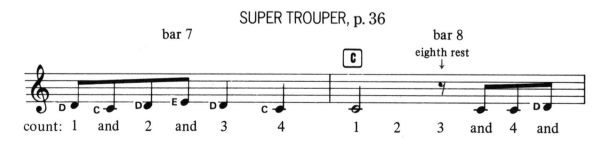

bar 7   bar 8

C   eighth rest

count: 1 and 2 and 3   4   1   2   3 and 4 and

LEGATO AND STACCATO

31

Legato means "joined up", "connected". When you play legato, you move smoothly from finger to finger, leaving no gaps between notes.

Notes which are to be played legato are indicated on the music by a curved line, called a "slur", or "phrase mark":—

BIRDIE SONG/BIRDIE DANCE, p.37

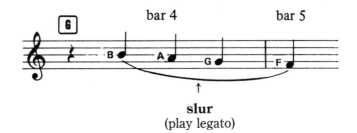

slur
(play legato)

When there are no slurs, or other markings to the contrary, assume that you are to play legato.

Staccato means "cut short". It is the opposite of "legato". Release the note as soon as you have played it, using a "pecking" movement of the hand.

Notes which are to be played staccato are indicated on the music by dots above, or below the note(s):—

BIRDIE SONG/BIRDIE DANCE, p. 37

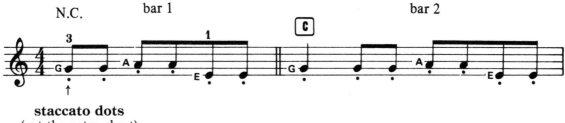

staccato dots
(cut the notes short)

SUPER TROUPER

Words & Music by Benny Andersson & Bjorn Ulvaeus

Suggested registration: *guitar*

Rhythm: rock
Tempo: medium (♩ = 116)

BIRDIE SONG/BIRDIE DANCE

Words & Music by Werner Thomas & Terry Rendall

Suggested registration: banjo

Rhythm: cha-cha (or rock)
Tempo: medium (♩ = 120)
Synchro-start, if available

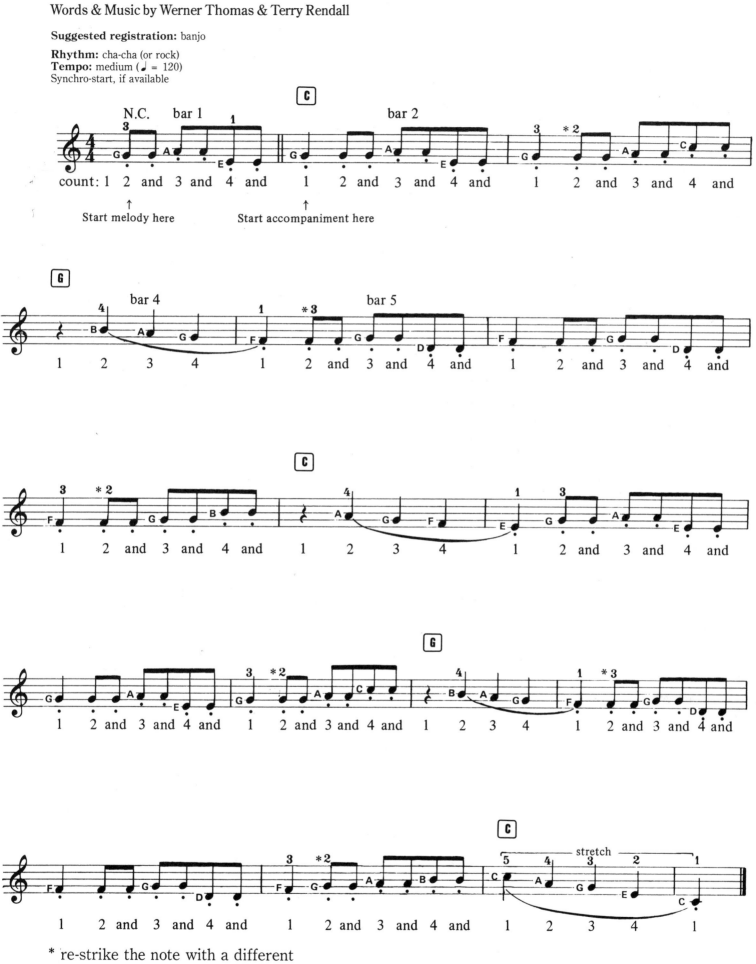

* re-strike the note with a different
finger, as shown.

32

ANNIE'S SONG

Words & Music by John Denver

Suggested registration: flute

Rhythm: waltz
Tempo: moderately fast (♩ = 132)
Synchro-start, if available

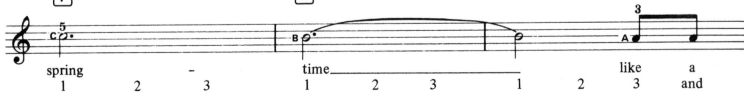

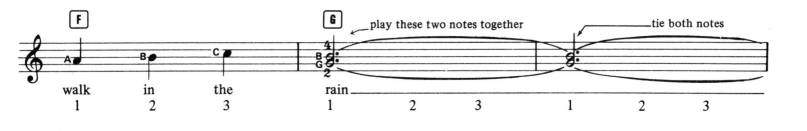

walk in the rain

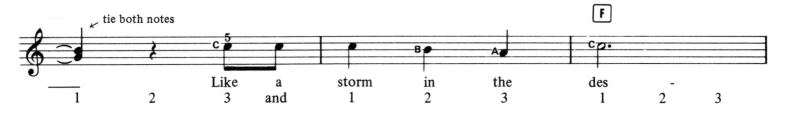

Like a storm in the des-

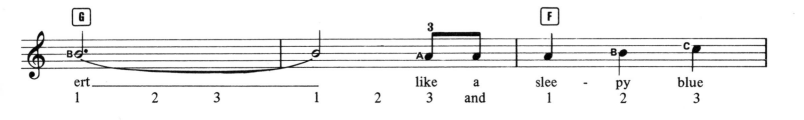

ert like a slee - py blue

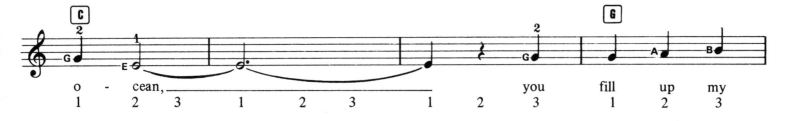

o - cean, you fill up my

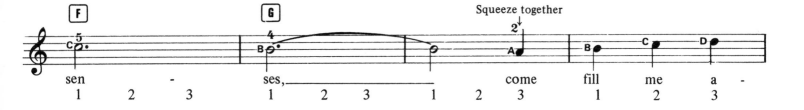

sen - ses, come fill me a -

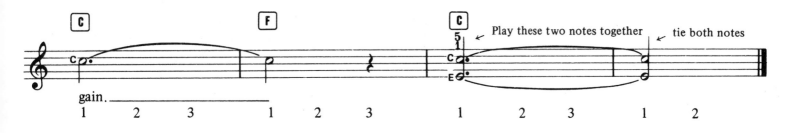

gain.

RIVERS OF BABYLON

Words & Music by Farian, Reyam, Dowe & McMaughton

Suggested registration: string ensemble + rock guitar

Rhythm: reggae (or rock)
Tempo: medium (♩ = 118)
Synchro-start, if available

* Section Lines. An old section is
over, and a new section is about to begin.

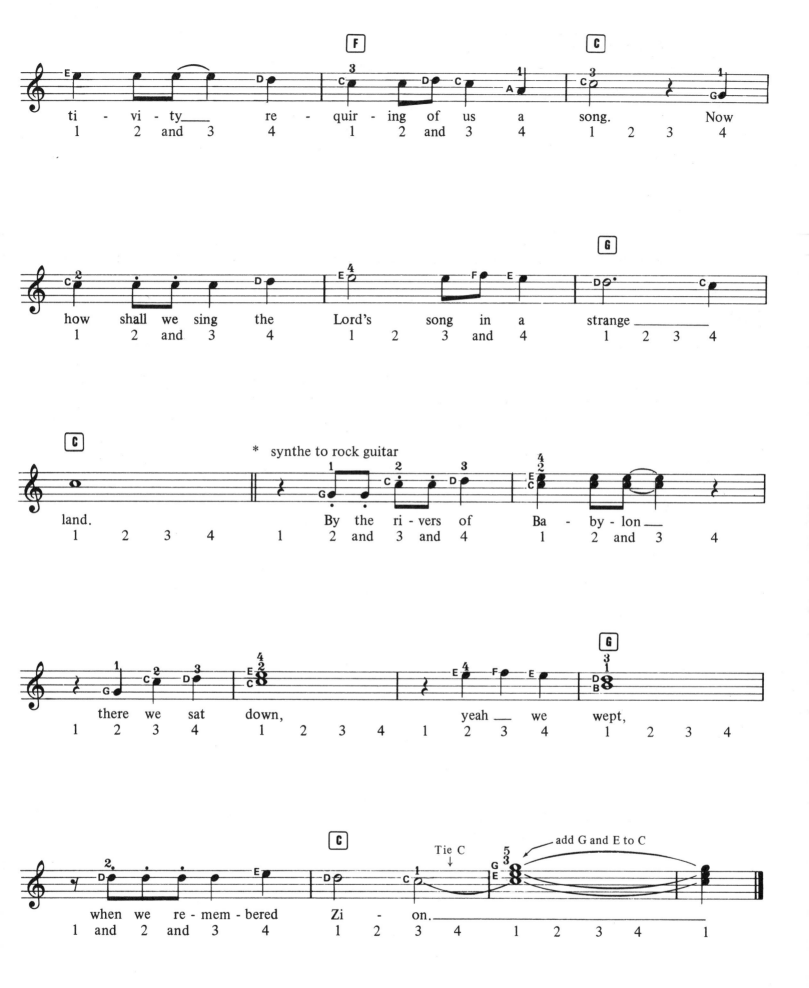

SEVENTH CHORDS

33

The three chords you have played so far: C, G, and F, are all "major" chords.

"Seventh" chords are variations of major chords.

When using the "single-finger chord" method, there are various ways of forming "sevenths". Your owner's manual will tell you exactly how to form 7ths on your particular instrument. However, the first two diagrams in 34, below, show two possibilities:

CHORD OF G7

34

Using single-finger chord method:

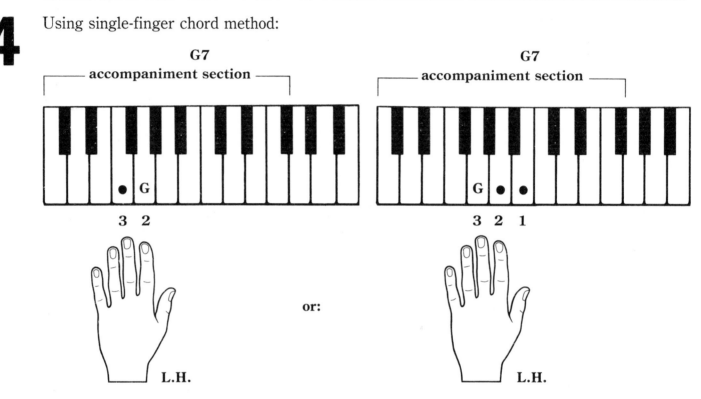

or:

play G, together with any white note to its LEFT.

play G, together with any two notes to its RIGHT

Using fingered chord method:

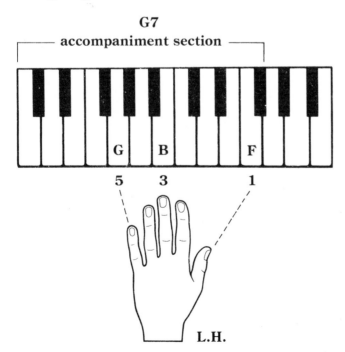

CHORD OF D7

35

Using single-finger chord method:

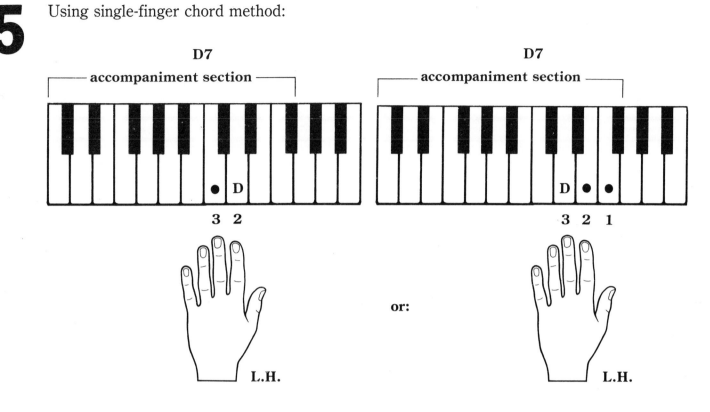

play D, together with any white note to its LEFT.

or:

play D, together with any two notes to its RIGHT.

Using fingered chord method:

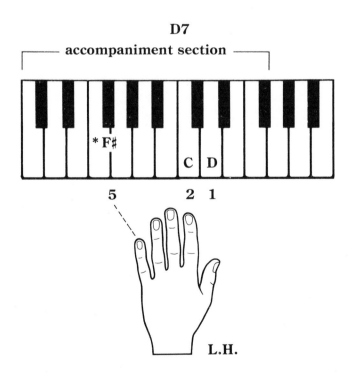

* Sharps and flats will be explained in Book Two. For now simply play the black note indicated.

EDELWEISS

Words by Oscar Hammerstein II
Music by Richard Rodgers

Suggested registration: string ensemble
(or violin solo). Arpeggio optional.
Rhythm: waltz
Tempo: fairly slow (♩ = 80)

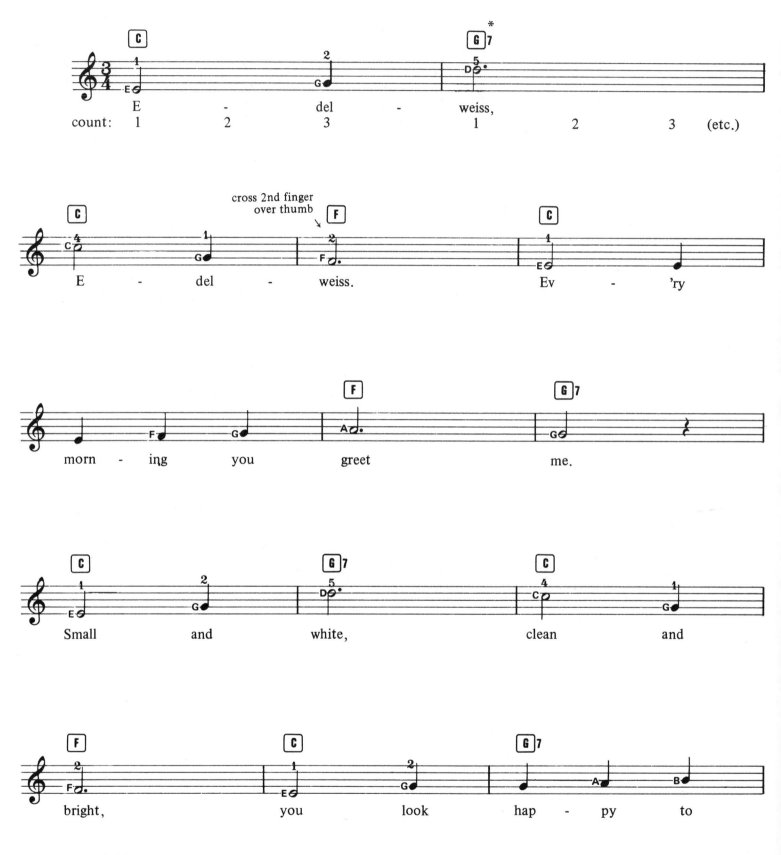

* If you are using the single-finger chord
method and have no 7th chords available
on your model, play "G",

36

Dal Segno means "repeat from the sign". The sign looks like this: 𝄋

Fine is the end of the piece.

Dal Segno Al Fine (D.S. al Fine) means go back to the sign: 𝄋 , play through the same music as before until you reach the word "Fine", which is the end of the piece.

I'D LIKE TO TEACH THE WORLD TO SING

Words and Music by Roger Cook, Roger Greenaway, Billy Backer & Billy Davis

Suggested registration: vibraphone + sustain

Rhythm: swing
Tempo: medium (♩ = 120)
Synchro-start, if available

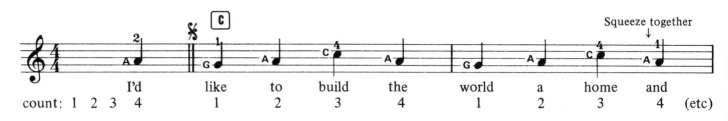

count: 1 2 3 4

I'd like to build the world a home and (etc)

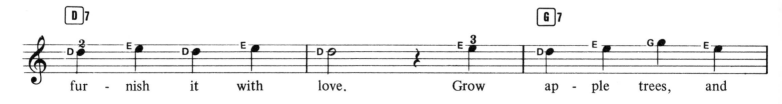

fur - nish it with love. Grow ap - ple trees, and

hon - ey bees, and snow - white tur - tle doves. I'd

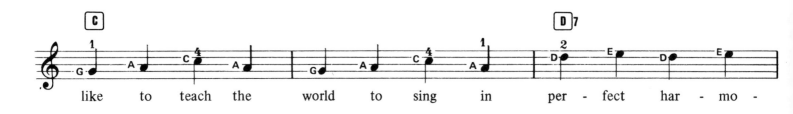

like to teach the world to sing in per - fect har - mo -

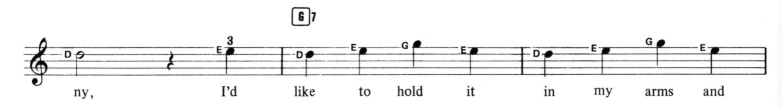

ny, I'd like to hold it in my arms and

* The SELECT, or SELECTOR button (in
  the melody section of your instrument),
  will change the sound from "vibraphone"
  to some other voice (depending on your
  model). Pressing the selector button is
  one of the easiest ways of making a
  registration change.

LAST WORD

37 So we come to the end of Book One of The Complete Keyboard Player. I am sure you are delighted with your progress so far.

In Book Two you will—

- learn about sharps and flats.

- increase the range of your melody playing.

- learn new chords, including minor chords.

- experiment with new sounds and rhythms.

Till then your last piece in this book is:

LET IT BE

Words & Music by John Lennon & Paul McCartney

Suggested registration: piano, or electric guitar

Rhythm: rock
Tempo: slow (♩ = 66)
Synchro-start, if available

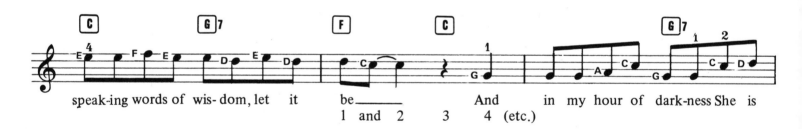

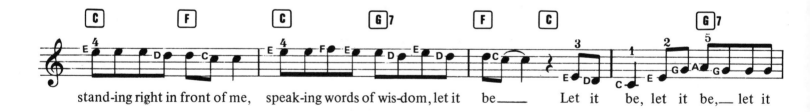

For all portable keyboards *by Kenneth Baker.*

THE COMPLETE KEYBOARD PLAYER

OMNIBUS EDITION

BOOK 2

In Book Two of The Complete Keyboard Player you take a giant step forward in reading musical notation.

Side by side with the single-finger chords, you continue your study of "fingered" chords, by far the most rewarding aspect of left hand accompaniment playing.

As the book progresses you play more and more fill-ins, double notes, and chords with your right hand, which helps give you that "professional" sound.

Although Book Two (like Book One of the series) is designed basically as a "teach yourself" method, teachers everywhere will find it ideal for training tomorrow's electronic keyboard players.

SHARPS, FLATS, AND NATURALS

1

This sign is a sharp: ♯

When you see a sharp written alongside a note, play the nearest available key (black or white) to the RIGHT of that note:—

written:

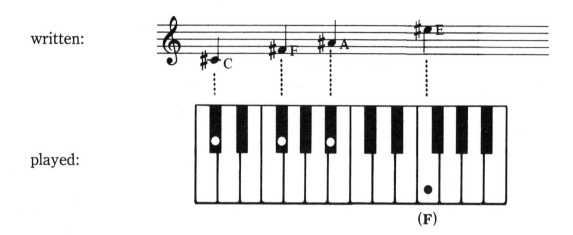

played:

(F)

Note: E sharp is simply an alternative way of writing "F".

This sign is a flat: ♭

When you see a flat written alongside a note, play the nearest available key (black or white) to the LEFT of that note:—

written:

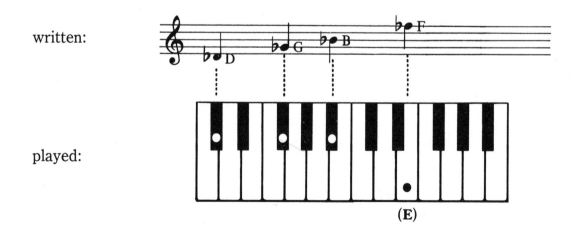

played:

(E)

Note: F flat is simply an alternative way of writing "E".

When a sharp or flat is written it
continues as a sharp or flat right through
the bar:—

At the next bar, however, everything
returns to normal:—

Apart from at the new bar, a sharp or flat
may be cancelled any time by a sign
called a "natural", ♮ :—

Look out for sharps, flats, and naturals in
the pieces which follow.

GET BACK

Words & Music by John Lennon & Paul McCartney

Suggested registration: electric guitar

Rhythm: rock
Tempo: medium (♩ = 120)

* **Common Time.** An alternative way of writing 4/4

* **Pause (Fermata).** Hold the note(s) longer
than written (at the discretion of the performer).

FOR ONCE IN MY LIFE

Words by Ronald Miller
Music by Orlando Murden

Suggested registration: piano + string
ensemble.   Arpeggio optional

Rhythm: samba
Tempo: medium (♩ = 108)
Synchro-start, if available

count: 1   2   3   4   1   2   and   3   4   and   1   2   and   3   and   4   (etc.)

For once in my life I have some - one who needs me ———

some - one I've need - ed so long.   For once un - a - fraid I can

go where life leads me, and some - how I know I'll be strong.   For

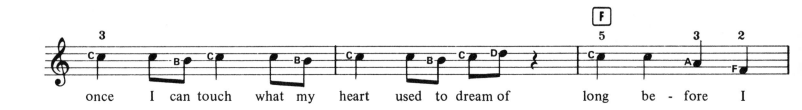

once I can touch what my heart used to dream of   long be - fore I

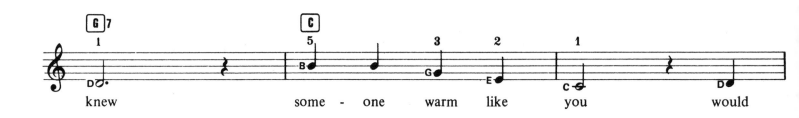

knew   some - one warm like you   would

ROCK AROUND THE CLOCK

Words & Music by Max C. Freedman & Jimmy
de Knight

Suggested registration: trumpet, or saxophone
Rhythm: swing
Tempo: fairly fast (♩ = 160)

Press rhythm start button (ordinary, not
synchro) with left hand, as right hand
strikes first note. Play through Verse
using melody and drums only. Start left
hand chords at Chorus.

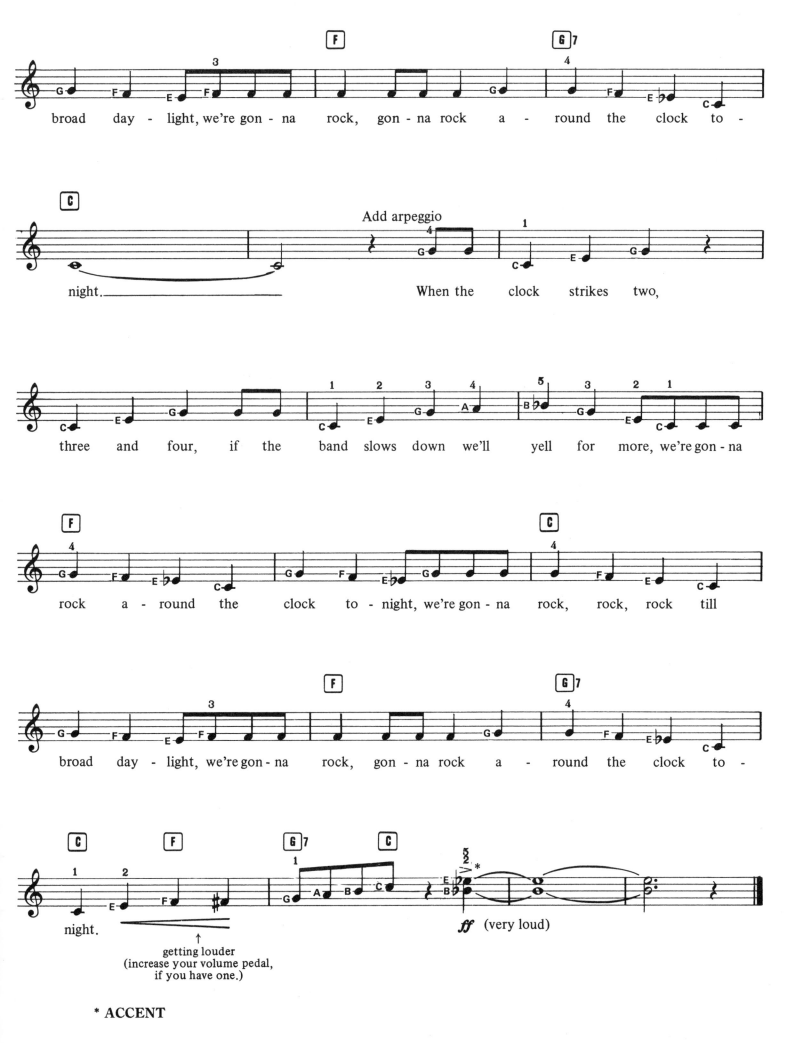

TWO NEW CHORDS: C7 AND A7

2

Using single-finger chord method:

Locate "C" and "A" in the accompaniment section of your keyboard. Convert these notes into "C7" and "A7" (see Book One, p. 42ff., and your owner's manual).

Using fingered chord method:

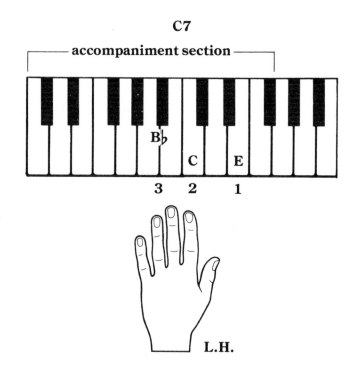

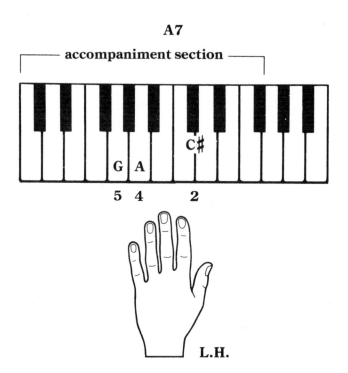

A NEW STAGE IN READING MUSIC

3 Up to now, in order to help you, letter names have appeared beside the written notes. These letters will now be discontinued.

Here's how you can learn the names of the notes:

The stave consists of five lines:—

remember this sentence:
Every Good Boy Deserves Fruit

and four spaces:—

remember this word: **F A C E**

Learn the notes on the five lines, and the notes in the four spaces first. Then learn the "in-between" notes, like this:

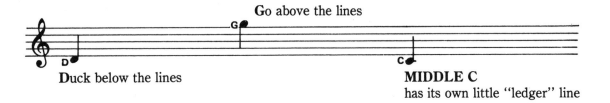

LET HIM GO, LET HIM TARRY

Traditional

Suggested registration: flute

Rhythm: bossa nova
Tempo: medium (♩ = 108)
Synchro-start, if available

Let him go, let him tar - ry, let him sink or let him

swim. He does - n't care for me, and

I don't care for him. He can go and get an -

oth - er that I hope he will en - joy. For

I'm going to mar - ry a far nic - er boy.

LOVE ME TENDER

Words & Music by Elvis Presley & Vera Matson

Suggested registration: string ensemble.
Arpeggio optional.

Rhythm: rock
Tempo: medium (♩ = 96)

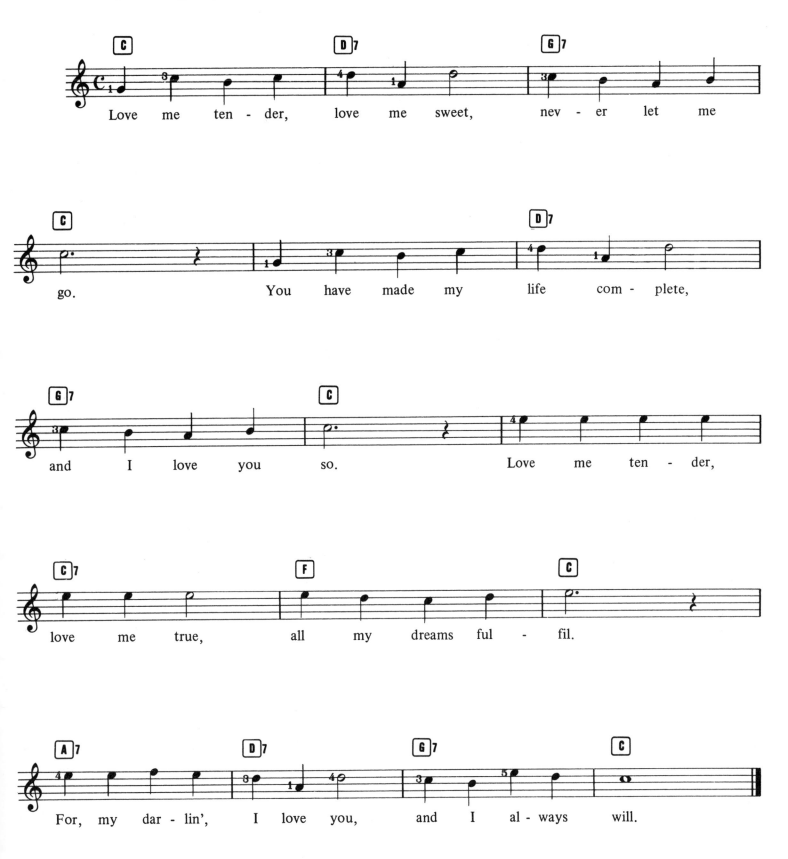

DAL SEGNO AL CODA (D.S. AL CODA)

4

A **Coda** is a section, usually quite short,
added to a piece of music to make an
ending.

Dal Segno al Coda (D.S. al Coda)
means go back to the sign: 𝄋 and play
through the same music again, until:

to coda ⊕

From here jump to CODA and play
through to the end.

SOMETHIN' STUPID

Words & Music by C. Carson Parks

Suggested registration: accordion

Rhythm: cha-cha (or rhumba)
Tempo: medium (♩ = 112)
Synchro-start, if available

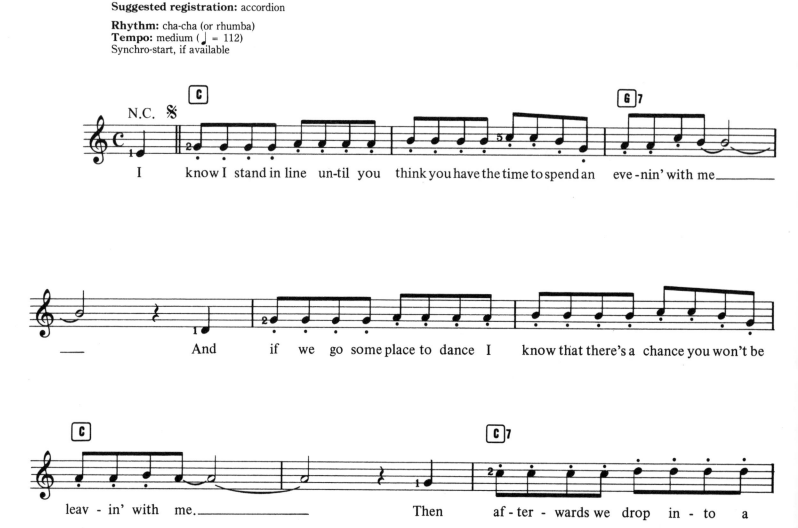

I know I stand in line un-til you think you have the time to spend an eve-nin' with me____

____ And if we go some place to dance I know that there's a chance you won't be

leav-in' with me._____ Then af-ter-wards we drop in-to a

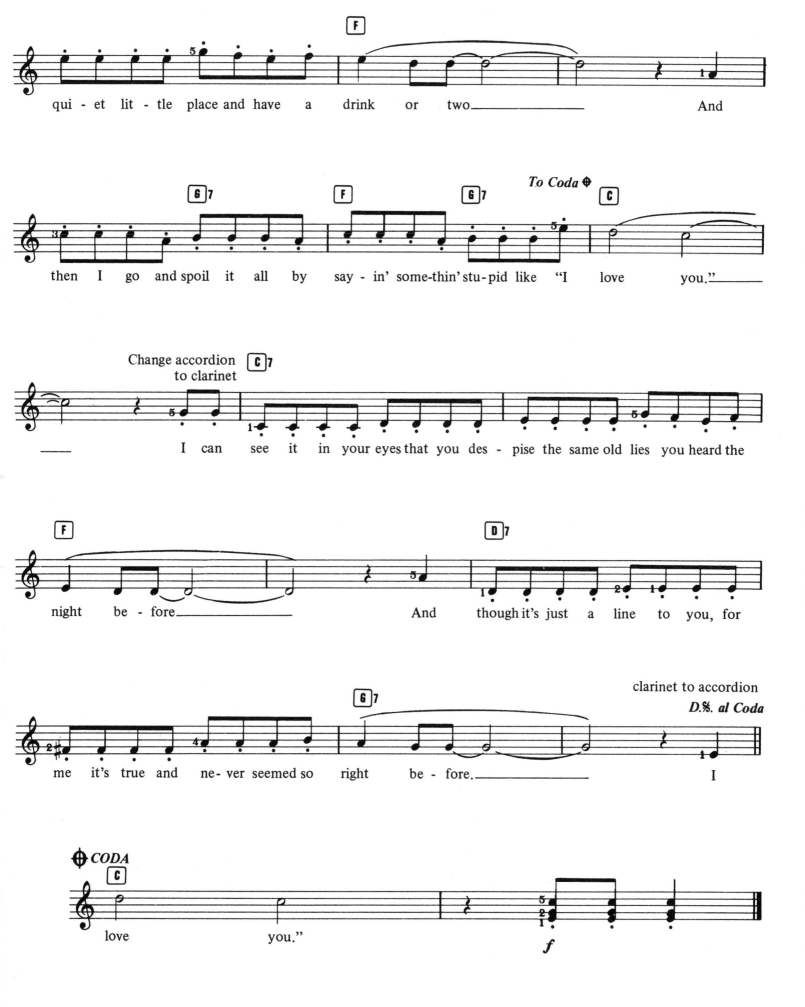

qui - et lit - tle place and have a drink or two_____ And

then I go and spoil it all by say - in' some-thin' stu - pid like "I love you."_____

Change accordion to clarinet

_____ I can see it in your eyes that you des - pise the same old lies you heard the

night be - fore._____ And though it's just a line to you, for

clarinet to accordion

me it's true and ne-ver seemed so right be - fore._____ I

CODA

love you." f

ARE YOU LONESOME TONIGHT

Words & Music by Roy Turk & Lou Handman

Suggested registration: flute + full sustain

Rhythm: waltz
Tempo: fairly slow (♩ = 80)
Synchro-start, if available

Are you lone - some to - night, do you miss me to - night, are you sor - ry we drift - ed a - part? Does your mem - or - y stray to a bright sum - mer day, when I kissed you and called you "Sweet -

Tuck thumb under 2nd finger

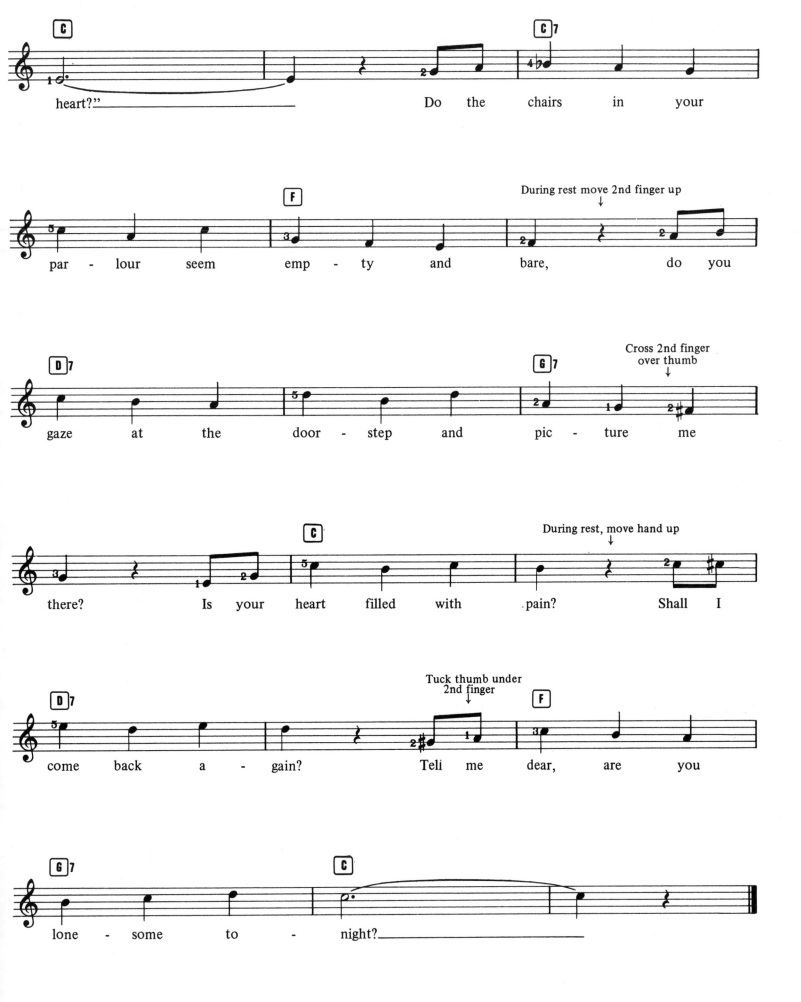

AN APPLE FOR THE TEACHER

Words by Johnny Burke
Music by James V. Monaco

Suggested registration: trombone, or horn

Rhythm: swing
Tempo: fairly fast (♩ = 176)
Synchro-start, if available

An ap - ple for the teach - er, that

seems the thing to do, be - cause I need to

learn a - bout ro - mance from you. An

ap - ple for the teach - er, to show I'm meek and

mild. If you in - sist on say - ing that I'm

THREE NEW NOTES FOR RIGHT HAND:
LOW G, A, B

5

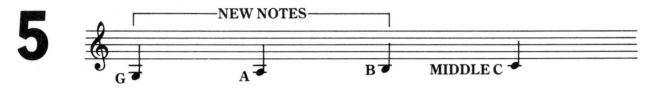

These three notes lie directly to the left of Middle C. The lowest of them, G, probably forms the left hand extremity of the "melody section" on your instrument.

I have placed letter names beside the new notes only in the next few songs.

GUANTANAMERA

Words by Jose Marti
Music adaptation by Hector Angulo & Pete Seeger

Suggested registration: flute, + duet (if available)

Rhythm: bossa nova
Tempo: medium (♩ = 100)

BILL BAILEY WON'T YOU PLEASE COME HOME

Traditional

Suggested registration: piano, or honky-tonk piano

Rhythm: swing
Tempo: fairly fast (♩ = 176)

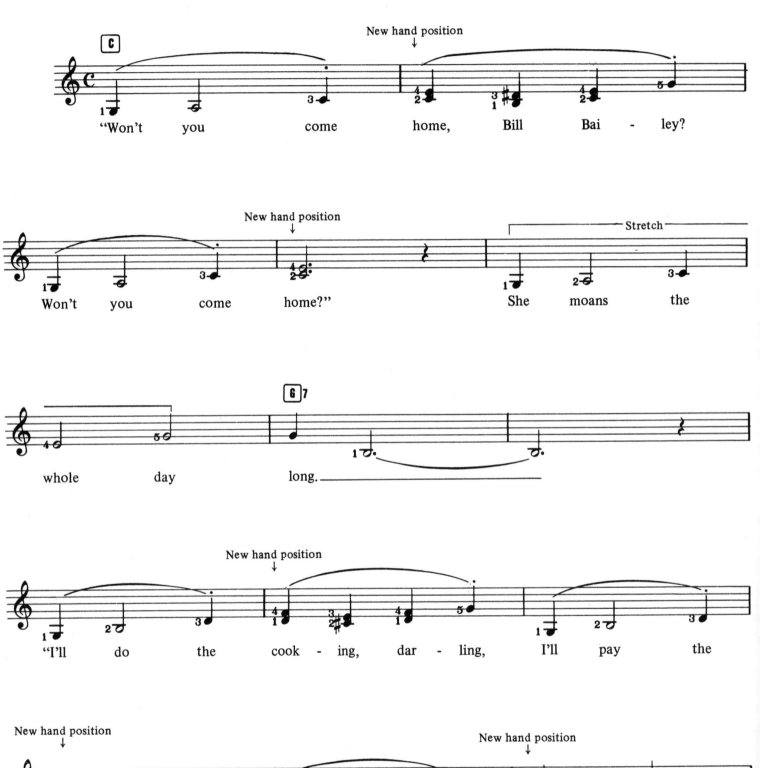

DA CAPO AL CODA (D.C. AL CODA)

6 **Da Capo** means "from the beginning".

Da Capo al Coda (D.C. al Coda) means go back to the beginning of the piece and play through the same music

again, until: to coda ⊕

From here jump to CODA and play through to the end.

THIS NEARLY WAS MINE

Words by Oscar Hammerstein II
Music by Richard Rodgers

Suggested registration: string ensemble

Rhythm: waltz
Tempo: slow (♩ = 80)

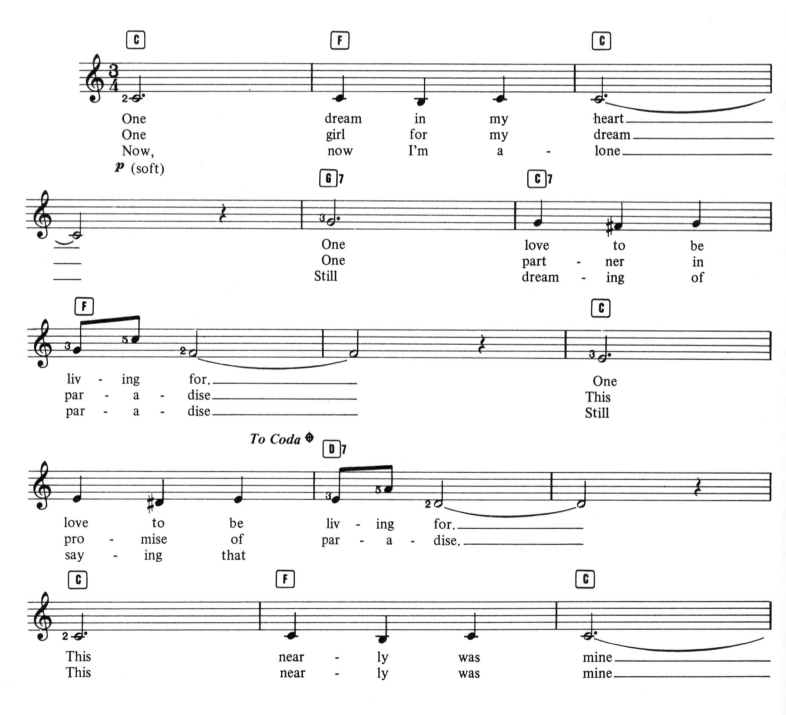

One	dream	in	my	heart
One	girl	for	my	dream
Now,	now	I'm	a - lone

p (soft)

One	love	to	be
One	part - ner	in
Still	dream - ing	of

liv - ing	for.	One
par - a - dise.	This
par - a - dise	Still

To Coda ⊕

love	to	be	liv - ing	for.
pro - mise	of	par - a - dise.
say - ing	that

| This | near - ly | was | mine |
| This | near - ly | was | mine |

72

MINOR CHORDS

7 The MINOR CHORD is another important type of chord.

When using the single-finger chord function, there are various ways of forming minor chords. Your owner's manual will tell you how to form minor chords on your particular instrument. The first two diagrams in 8, on the next page, show two possibilities.

CHORD OF F MINOR (Fm)

Using single-finger chord method:

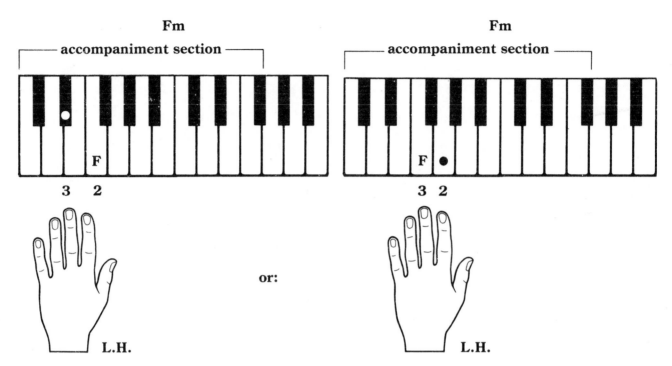

or:

play F, together with any black note to its LEFT.

play F, together with any (one) note to its RIGHT.

Using fingered chord method:

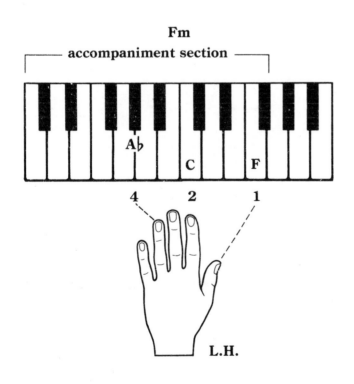

DOTTED TIME NOTES

 A dot after a note adds half as much time again to that note:—

		lasting
♩	half note (minim)	2 beats
♩.	dotted half note (dotted minim)	2 + 1 = 3 beats
♩	quarter note (crotchet)	1 beat
♩.	dotted quarter note (dotted crotchet)	1 + ½ = 1½ beats

DOTTED QUARTER NOTE (DOTTED CROTCHET)

10 A Dotted Quarter Note, ♩., worth 1½ beats, usually combines with an Eighth Note (Quaver), ♪, worth ½ beat, to make two whole beats:—

     ♩.   ♪   1½ + ½ = 2 beats

or: ♪   ♩.   ½ + 1½ = 2 beats

The first of these two time note combinations: ♩. ♪ is the more common. This is how you count it:—

WHAT KIND OF FOOL AM I, p. 76

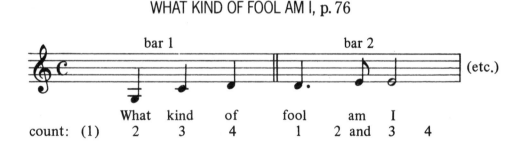

Notice how the "dot" delays note D, so that the next note (E) falls on an "and" beat. The situation is always the same with this rhythm.

Look out for other examples of dotted quarter note/quaver combinations in the songs which follow.

WHAT KIND OF FOOL AM I

Words & Music by Leslie Bricusse & Anthony Newley

Suggested registration: piano

Rhythm: bossa nova
Tempo: medium (♩ = 100)
Synchro-start, if available

LOVE'S ROUNDABOUT
(LA RONDE DE L'AMOUR)

French Words by Louis Ducreux
English Words by Harold Purcell
Music by Oscar Straus

Suggested registration: accordion
    + arpeggio (if available)

Rhythm: waltz
Tempo: fairly fast (♩ = 160)

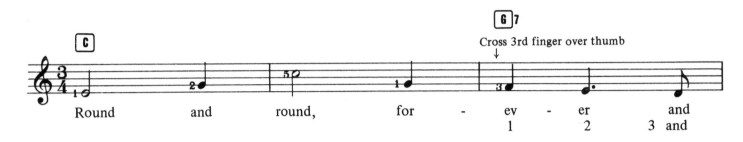

Cross 3rd finger over thumb

Round and round, for - ev - er and
1 2 3 and

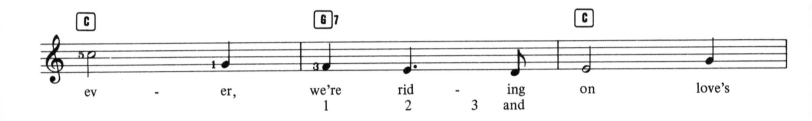

ev - er, we're rid - ing on love's
1 2 3 and

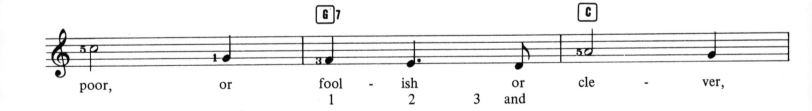

round - a - bout; rich or

poor, or fool - ish or cle - ver,
1 2 3 and

round we must go, year in, year
1 2 3 and

Change accordion to clarinet

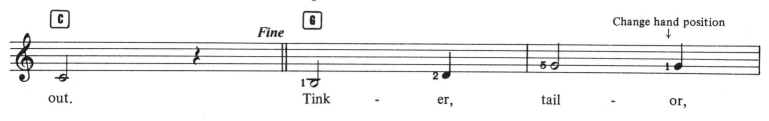

out.   Tink - er,   tail - or,

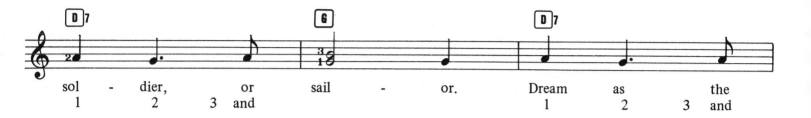

sol - dier,   or   sail - or.   Dream   as   the
1   2   3   and   1   2   3   and

world   goes   rid -   ing   by.

Turn   the   pag -   es   back   thro'   the
1   2   3   and

a -   ges;   what   are   their   names?   Just
1   2   3   and

Change clarinet to accordion
*D.C. al FINE

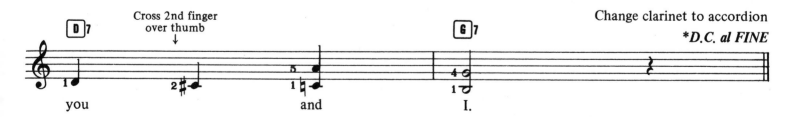

you   and   I.

* **Da Capo Al Fine.** Go back to the beginning
of the piece and play through the same music
again until FINE (the end).

STARDUST

Words by Mitchell Parish
Music by Hoagy Carmichael

Suggested registration: vibraphone, or celeste,
 + full sustain

Rhythm: swing
Tempo: fairly slow (♩ = 80)
Synchro-start, if available

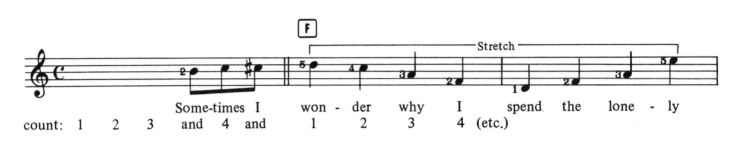

Some-times I won - der why I spend the lone - ly

count: 1 2 3 and 4 and 1 2 3 4 (etc.)

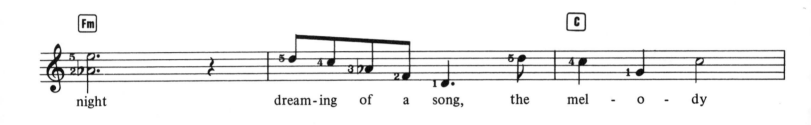

night dream-ing of a song, the mel - o - dy

haunts my re - ve - rie. And I am once a - gain with you. When our

love was new, and each kiss an in - spi - ra - tion

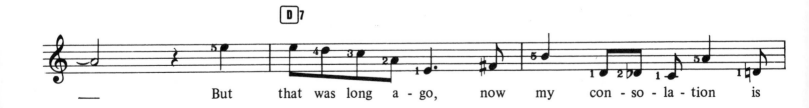

But that was long a - go, now my con - so - la - tion is

CHORD OF D MINOR (Dm), AND CHORD OF A MINOR (Am)

11 Using single-finger chord method:

Locate D (the higher one), and A, in the accompaniment section of your keyboard. Convert these notes into "Dm" and "Am" respectively (see Book Two, p. 74 and your owner's manual).

Using fingered chord method:

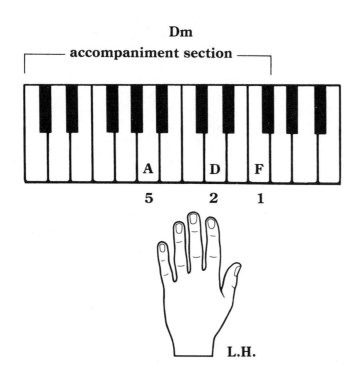

Dm

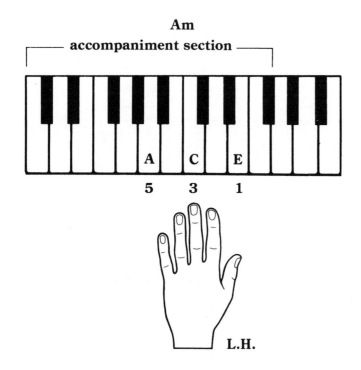

Am

SCARBOROUGH FAIR

Traditional

Suggested registration: flute

Rhythm: waltz
Tempo: slow (♩ = 84)

TAKE ME HOME, COUNTRY ROADS

Words & Music by Bill Danoff, Taffy Nivert &
John Denver

Suggested registration: piano, or electric piano
+ half sustain

Rhythm: swing
Tempo: quite fast (♩ = 192)

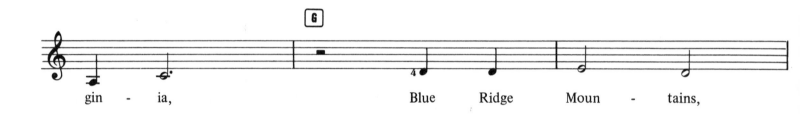

Al - most hea - ven, West Vir -

gin - ia, Blue Ridge Moun - tains,

Shen - an - do - ah Riv - er.

Life is old there, old - er than the

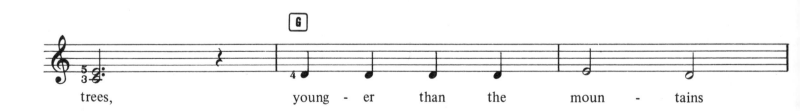

trees, young - er than the moun - tains

change piano to Hawaiian guitar (or electric guitar)

grow - in' like a breeze. Coun - try roads take me home to the place I be - long: West Vir - gin - ia moun - tain mom - ma, take me home coun - try roads.

12

If you have a 44, or a 49 note keyboard, these will be your top three notes.

I have placed letter names beside the new notes in the next few songs.

SAILING

Words & Music by Gavin Sutherland

Suggested registration: jazz organ
+ sustain

Rhythm: disco
Tempo: slow ($\quarternote$ = 69); but run rhythm at double speed ($\quarternote$ = 138)
Synchro-start, if available

* Pause on each note, for dramatic effect.

fly - ing,   I am fly - ing,   like a bird____   'cross the

f

sea.   I am fly - ing,   pass - ing high clouds,   to be

Add arpeggio (if available)

near____ you,   to be free.   We are sail - ing,   we are

ff

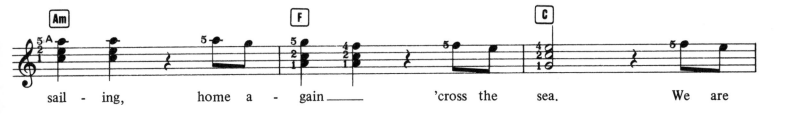

sail - ing,   home a - gain____ 'cross the sea.   We are

sail - ing storm - y wa - ters,   to be near____ you,   to be

Stop rhythm

free.   To be near____ you,   to be free.

SPANISH EYES

Words by Charles Singleton & Eddie Snyder
Music by Bert Kaempfert

Suggested registration: string ensemble

Rhythm: tango (or beguine)
Tempo: medium (♩ = 108)

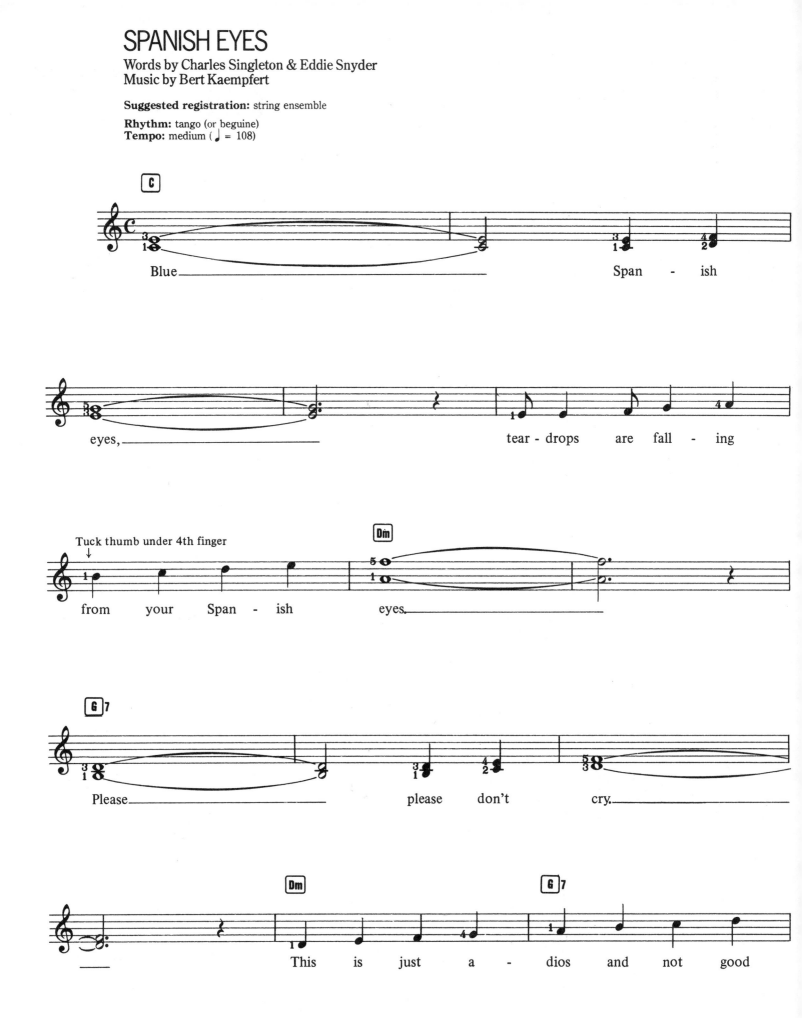

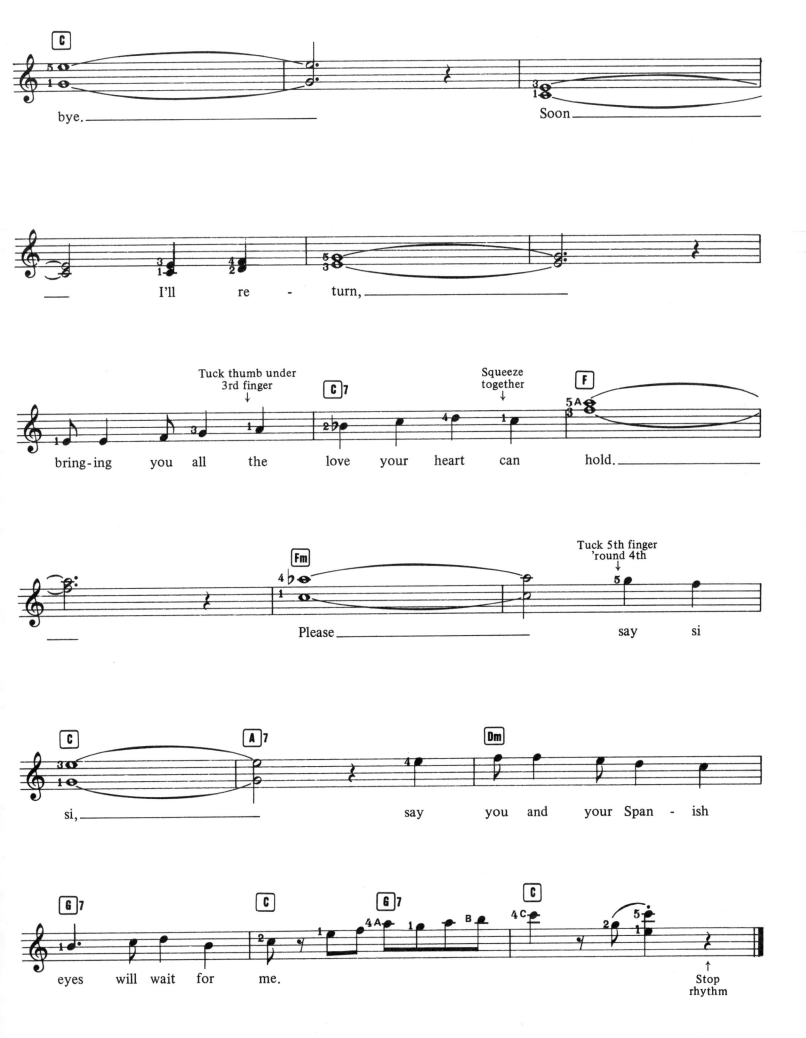

bye. _____ Soon _____

_____ I'll re - turn, _____

Tuck thumb under
3rd finger
↓

Squeeze
together
↓

bring-ing you all the love your heart can hold. _____

Tuck 5th finger
'round 4th
↓

Please _____ say si

si, _____ say you and your Span - ish

eyes will wait for me.

↑
Stop
rhythm

CRUISING DOWN THE RIVER

Words & Music by Eily Beadell & Nell Tollerton

Suggested registration: accordion

Rhythm: waltz
Tempo: fairly fast (♩ = 152)

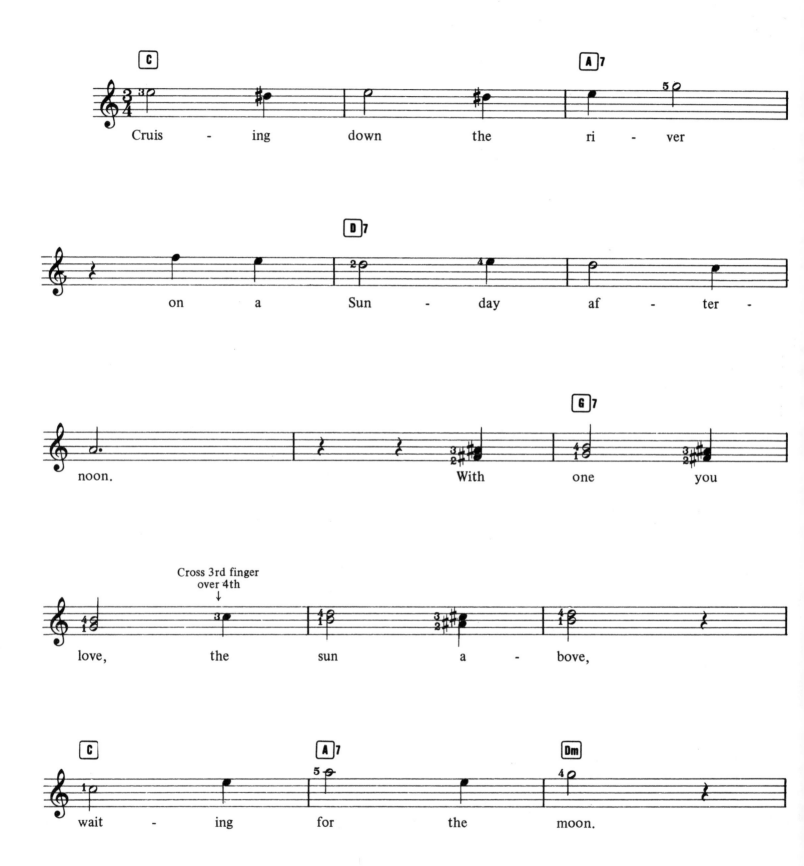

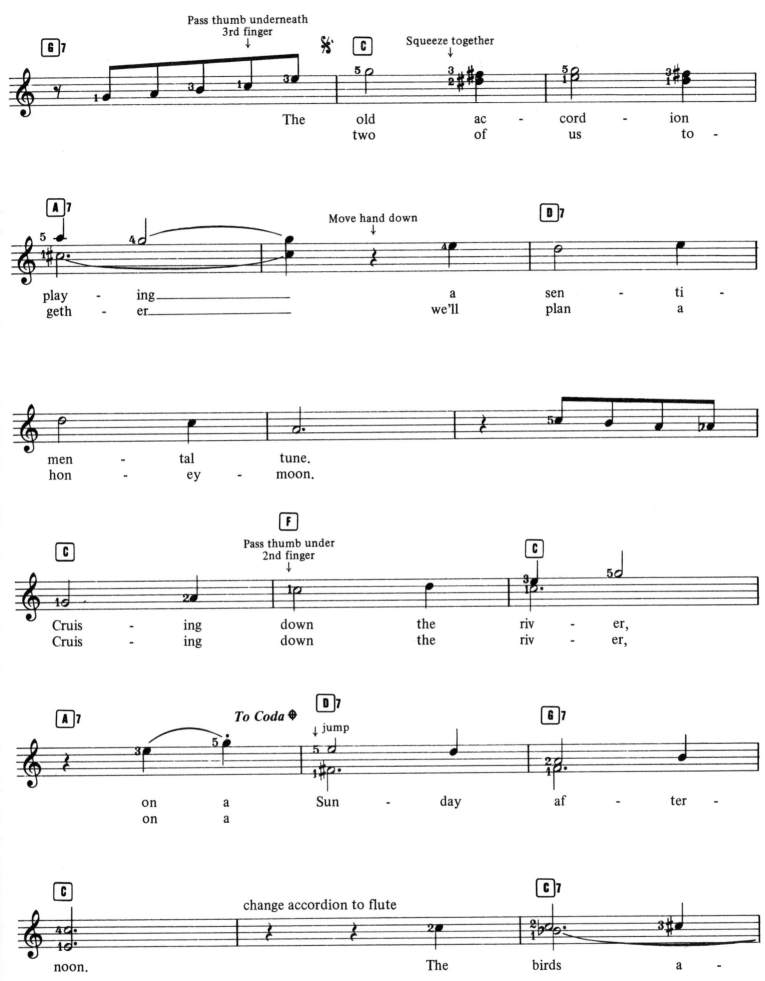

The old ac - cord - ion
two of us to -

play - ing_____ a sen - ti -
geth - er_____ we'll plan a

men - tal tune.
hon - ey - moon.

Cruis - ing down the riv - er,
Cruis - ing down the riv - er,

on a Sun - day af - ter -
on a

noon. The birds a -

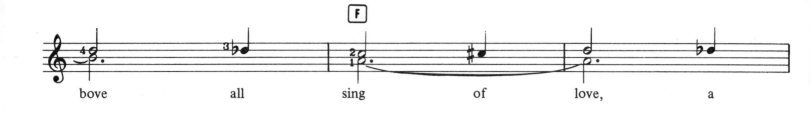

bove   all   sing   of   love,   a

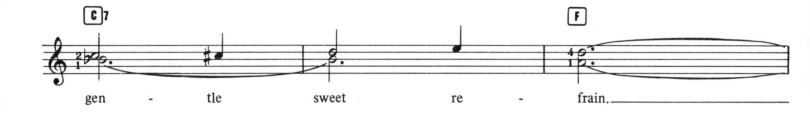

gen -   tle   sweet   re -   frain. _____

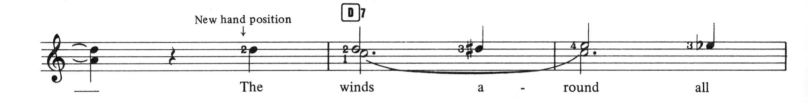

_____   The   winds   a -   round   all

New hand position

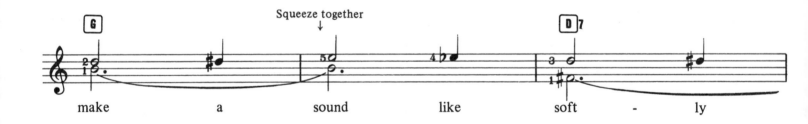

make   a   sound   like   soft -   ly

Squeeze together

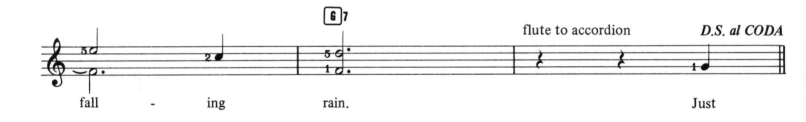

fall -   ing   rain.   Just

flute to accordion   *D.S. al CODA*

✛ *CODA*

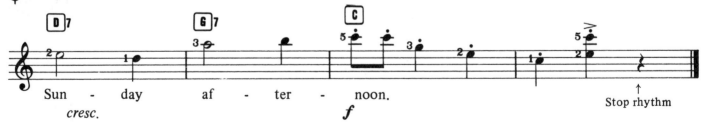

Sun -   day   af - ter -   noon.   Stop rhythm

cresc.   *f*

HELLO GOODBYE

Words & Music by John Lennon & Paul McCartney

Suggested registration: electric guitar

Rhythm: rock
Tempo: medium (♩ = 112)

LAST WORD

13 Congratulations on reaching the end of Book Two of The Complete Keyboard Player.

In Book Three you will

- improve your note reading
- learn new chords
- play in new keys, including "minor" keys
- develop further your sense of rhythm
- add those important professional touches to your playing.

CHORD CHART (Showing all "fingered chords" used in the course so far)

14

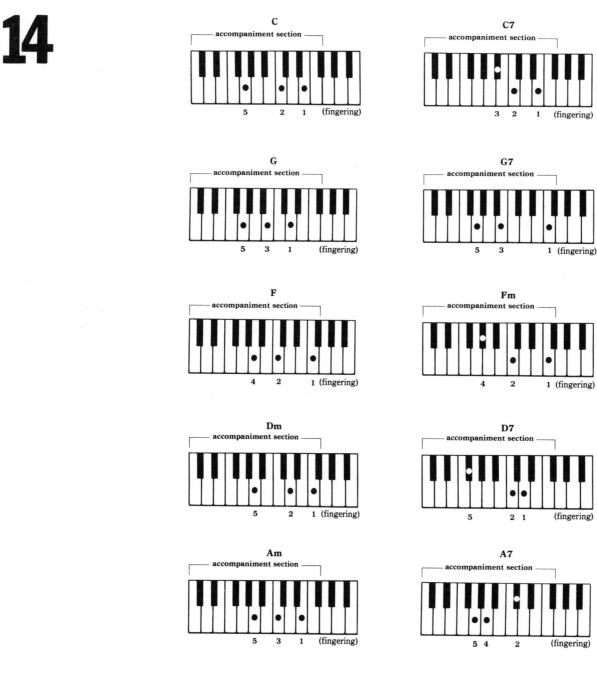

For all portable keyboards *by Kenneth Baker.*

THE COMPLETE KEYBOARD PLAYER

OMNIBUS EDITION

BOOK 3

In Book Three of The Complete Keyboard Player you learn about scales and keys. When you play in different keys you make basic changes of sound, and so add a new dimension to your playing. Minor keys, especially, can change the whole flavour of your music. In Book Three you play in five new keys, including two minor keys.

In Book Three you continue your left hand studies, with the emphasis as usual on "fingered" chords. Nine new chords are introduced, in easy stages, and all the chords used in the series appear in the Chord Chart at the back of the book.

There is plenty for your right hand in Book Three. There are double notes, chords, fill-ins, counter-melodies, and so on, and several new and effective tricks of the trade, such as ornamental "grace notes" and acciaccaturas.

As usual, throughout the book you will get tips on how to use the facilities of the keyboard — the sounds, the rhythms, and so on — more effectively.

Although Book Three continues in the "teach yourself" tradition of the earlier books, all teachers of the instrument will want to make it one of their standard text books.

CHORD OF E7

1 Using single-finger chord method:

Locate "E" (the higher one of two) in the accompaniment section of your keyboard. Convert this note into "E7" (see Book One, p. 42ff., and your owner's manual).

Using fingered chord method:

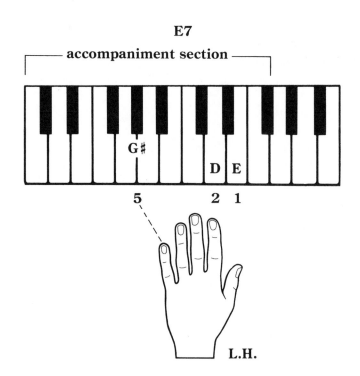

THE WINNER TAKES IT ALL

Words & Music by Benny Andersson &
Bjorn Ulvaeus

Suggested registration: piano

Rhythm: rock
Tempo: medium (♩ = 104)
Synchro-start, if available

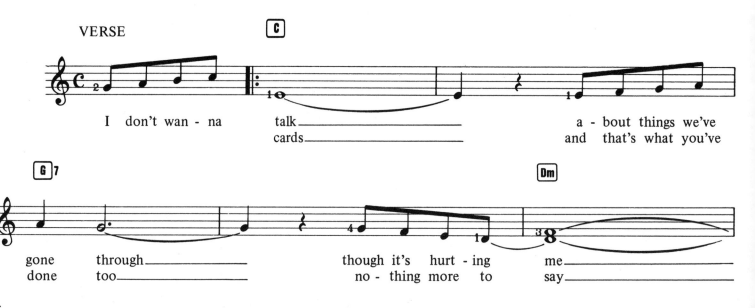

I don't wan - na talk_____ a - bout things we've
cards_____ and that's what you've

gone through_____ though it's hurt - ing me_____
done too_____ no - thing more to say_____

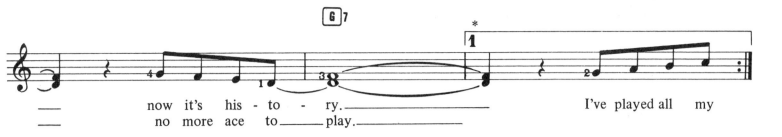

now it's his-to-ry._____
no more ace to_____play._____
I've played all   my

* 1st Time Bar. Play this bar on the first time through only (then repeat as marked).

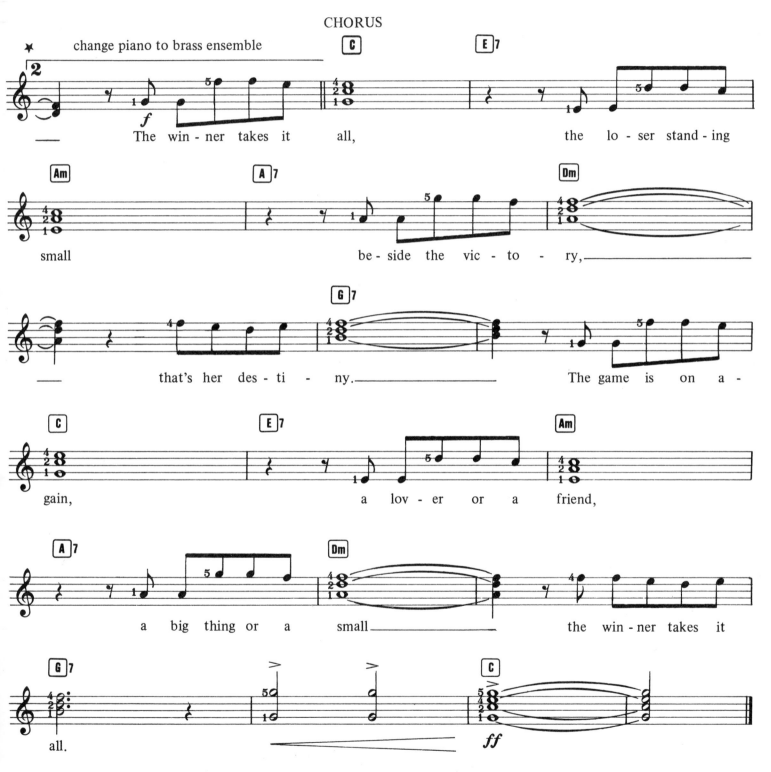

CHORUS

change piano to brass ensemble

The win-ner takes it   all,   the lo-ser stand-ing

small   be-side the vic-to-ry,_____

that's her des-ti-ny._____   The game is on a-

gain,   a lov-er or a   friend,

a big thing or a   small_____   the win-ner takes it

all.

✱ 2nd Time Bar. Play this bar on the second time through only (then carry on to the end).

I LEFT MY HEART IN SAN FRANCISCO

Words by Douglas Cross
Music by George Cory

Suggested registration: string ensemble

Rhythm: swing
Tempo: fairly slow (♩ = 88)
Synchro-start, if available

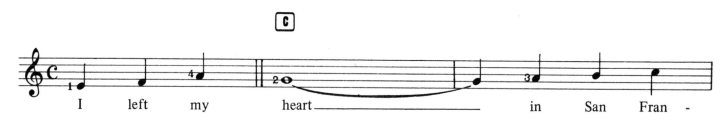

I left my heart _____ in San Fran -

cis - co. High on a hill

it calls to me. To be where

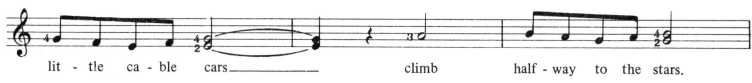

lit - tle ca - ble cars _____ climb half - way to the stars.

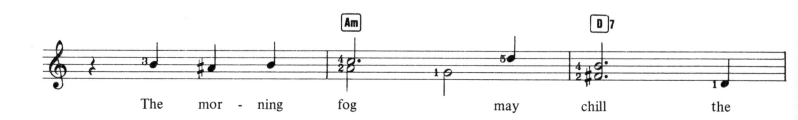

The mor - ning fog may chill the

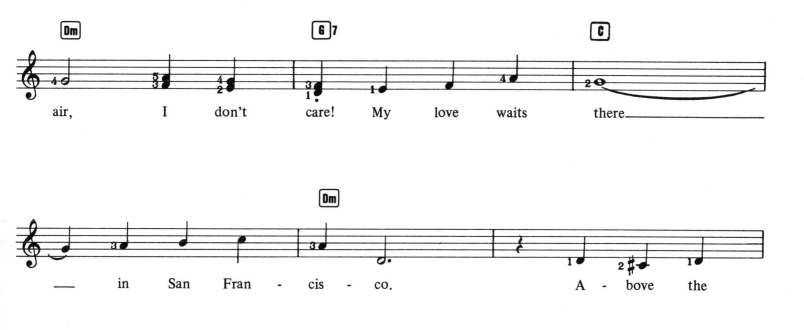

air, I don't care! My love waits there ___

___ in San Fran - cis - co. A - bove the

blue and wind - y sea.

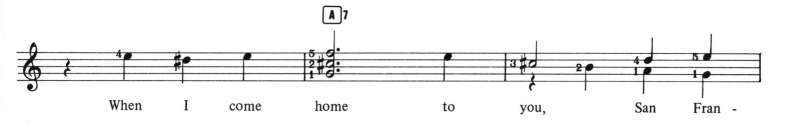

When I come home to you, San Fran -

cis - co. Your gold - en sun will

shine for me.

CHORD OF E MINOR (Em)

2 Using single-finger chord method:

Locate E (the higher one of two) in the accompaniment section of your keyboard. Convert this note into "Em" (see Book Two, p. 74, and your owner's manual).

Using fingered chord method:

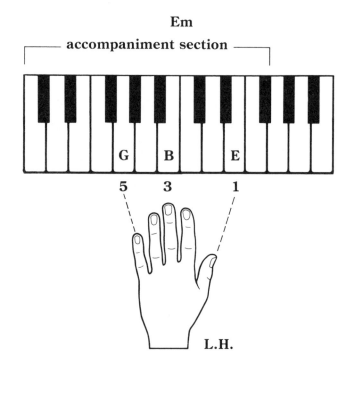

BRIGHT EYES
Words & Music by Mike Batt

Suggested registration:
electric guitar + arpeggio

Rhythm: rock
Tempo: medium (♩ = 96)

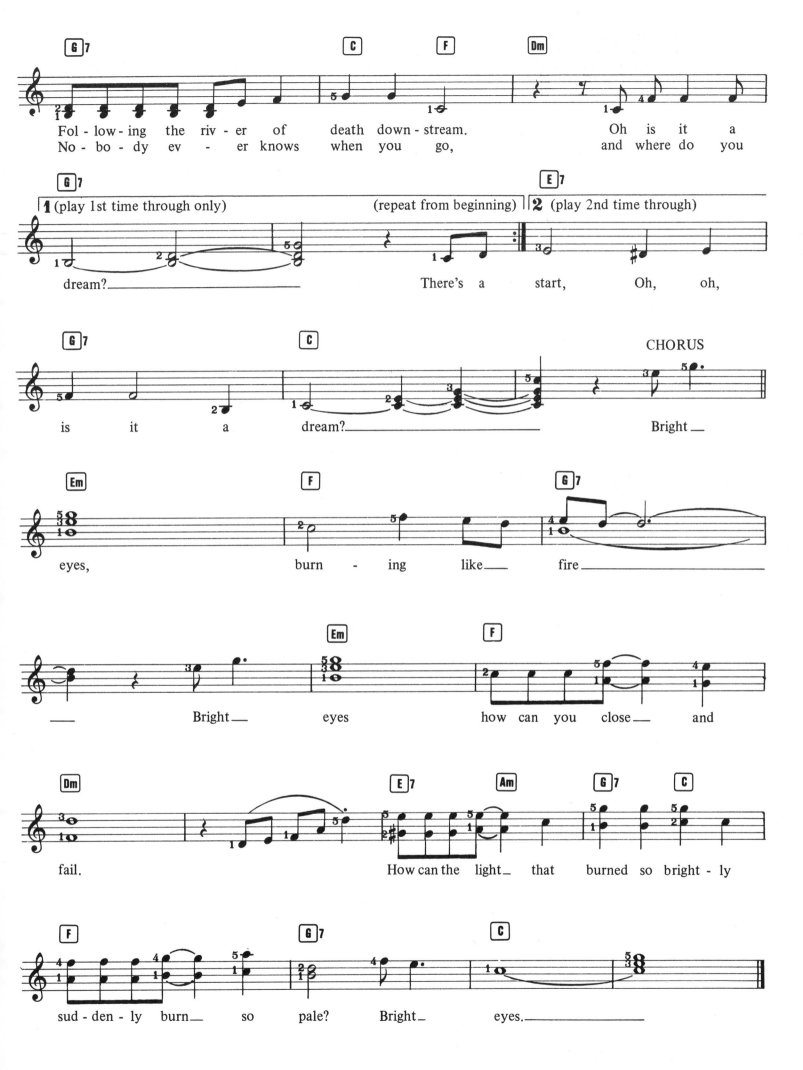

THE SONG FROM "MOULIN ROUGE"

(WHERE IS YOUR HEART?)

Words by William Engvick
Music by Georges Auric

Suggested registration: hawaiian
guitar

Rhythm: waltz
Tempo: slow (♩ = 80)
Synchro-start, if available

When - ev - er we kiss, I

wor - ry and won - der, your lips may be

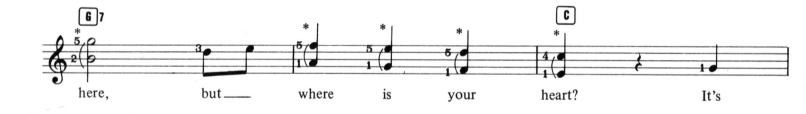

here, but___ where is your heart? It's

al - ways like this, I wor - ry and

won - der, you're close to me here, but___

*split these two notes (playing lower note
first).

where is your heart? It's a sad thing to re - al -

ise that you've a heart that nev - er melts. _____ When we

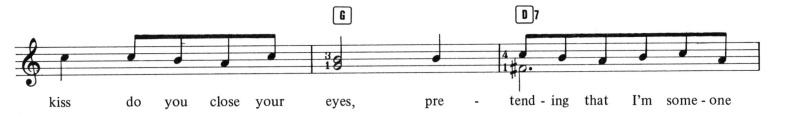

kiss do you close your eyes, pre - tend - ing that I'm some - one

else? You must break the spell, this

cloud that I'm un - der, so please won't you

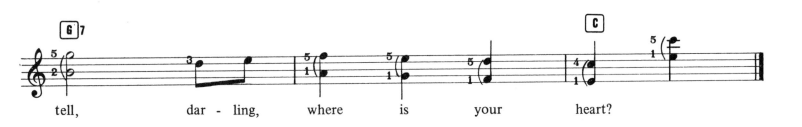

tell, dar - ling, where is your heart?

SCALE OF C; KEY OF C

3

A scale is a succession of adjoining notes:

Scale of C (major)

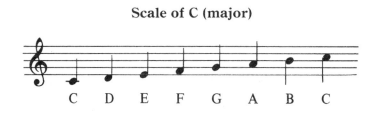

C   D   E   F   G   A   B   C

As you see, there are no black notes in the scale of C.

When a piece is built on this scale it is said to be in the "key of C". Almost all the pieces you have played so far have been in the key of C. The occasional black notes you encountered in those pieces were of a temporary nature only, and did not affect the overall key.

From now on you are going to play in a number of different keys for the sake of contrast.

SCALE OF F; KEY OF F

4

Scale of F (major)

F   G   A   (B♭)   C   D   E   F

As you see, a B Flat is required to form the scale of F. When you are playing in this key, therefore, you must remember to play all your B's, wherever they might fall on the keyboard, as B Flats.
To remind you, a B Flat is inserted at the beginning of every line:—

key signature

To help you further, I have arrowed the first few B Flats in the following songs.

CHORD OF B♭; CHORD OF F7

5

You need these two chords in order to play in the Key of F.

Using single-finger chord method:

Locate "B♭" in the accompaniment section of your keyboard. Play this note on its own and you will have a chord of

B♭ (major).

Locate "F" (the lower one of two) in the accompaniment section of your keyboard. Convert this into "F7" (see Book One, p. 42ff., and your owner's manual).

Using fingered chord method:

B♭

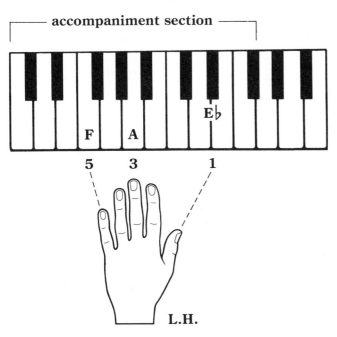

F7

OB-LA-DI, OB-LA-DA

Words & Music by John Lennon & Paul McCartney

Suggested registration: funny

Rhythm: swing
Tempo: fast ($\quad$ = 112)

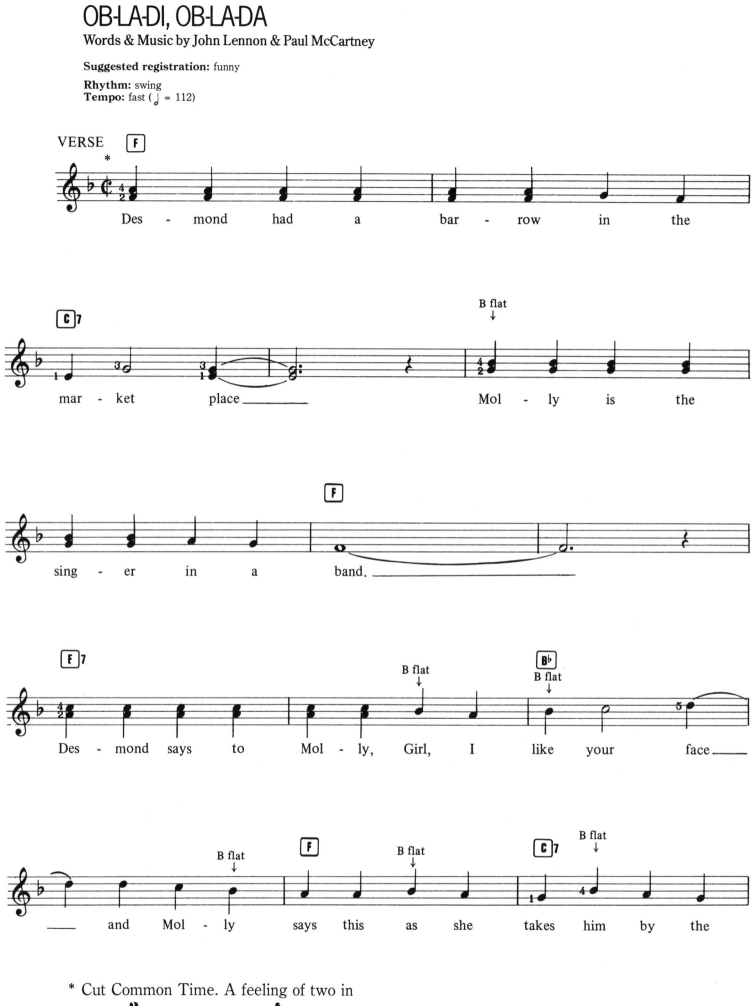

VERSE

Des - mond had a bar - row in the mar - ket place _____ Mol - ly is the sing - er in a band. _____

Des - mond says to Mol - ly, Girl, I like your face _____ and Mol - ly says this as she takes him by the

* Cut Common Time. A feeling of two in
a bar ($\mathbf{2 \atop 2}$) rather than four ($\mathbf{4 \atop 4}$). Notice the
metronome marking: $\quad$ = 112.

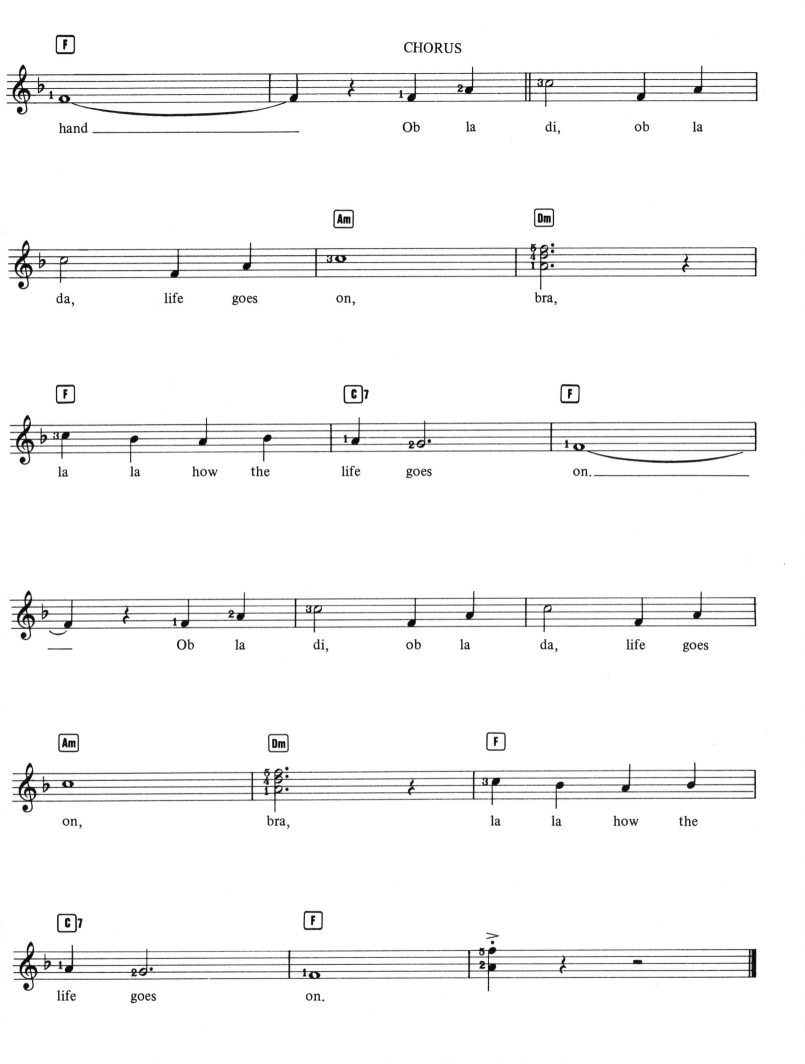

TIME ON MY HANDS

Words by Harold Adamson & Mack Gordon
Music by Vincent Youmans

Suggested registration: string
ensemble

Rhythm: swing
Tempo: slow (♩ = 84)

Time   on   my   hands.

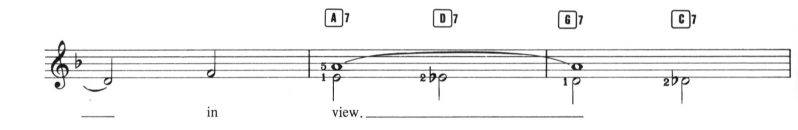

You   in   my   arms.   No-thing   but   love _____

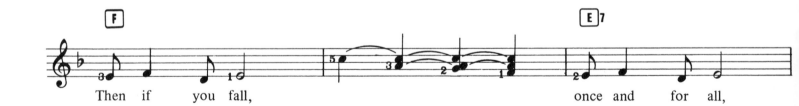

_____   in   view. _____

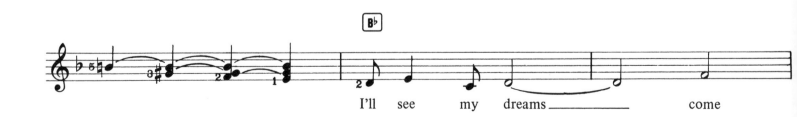

Then   if   you   fall,   once   and   for   all,

I'll   see   my   dreams _____   come

true. _____ Mo - ments to spare _____

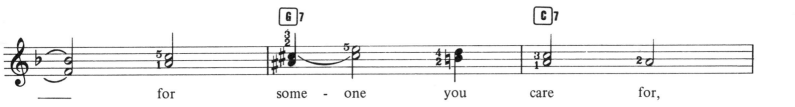

_____ for some - one you care for,

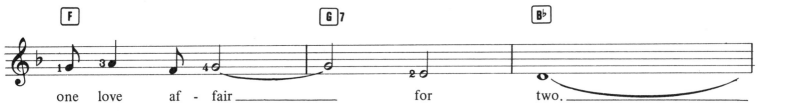

one love af - fair _____ for two. _____

_____ With time on my hands, and

you in my arms, _____ and love in my heart

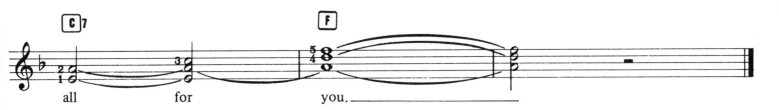

all for you. _____

TULIPS FROM AMSTERDAM

English Words by Gene Martyn
Original Words by Neumann and Bader
Music by Ralf Arnie

Suggested registration: accordion

Rhythm: waltz
Tempo: fast (♩ = 184)
Synchro-start, if available

When it's spring a - gain, I'll

bring a - gain Tu - lips from

Am - ster - dam. With a

heart that's true I'll give to you

Tu - lips from Am - ster - dam. I can't

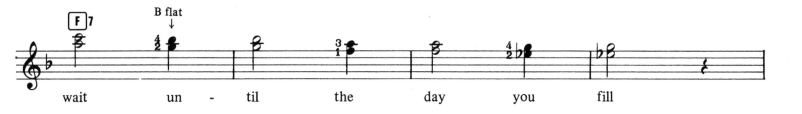

wait   un - til   the   day   you   fill

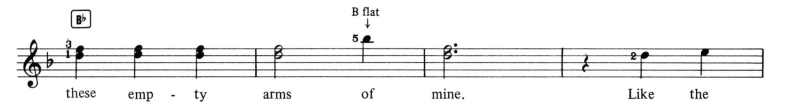

these   emp - ty   arms   of   mine.   Like   the

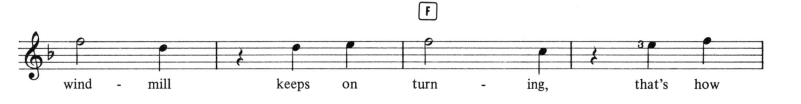

wind - mill   keeps   on   turn - ing,   that's   how

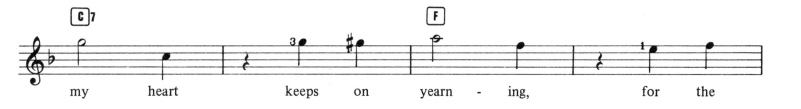

my   heart   keeps   on   yearn - ing,   for   the

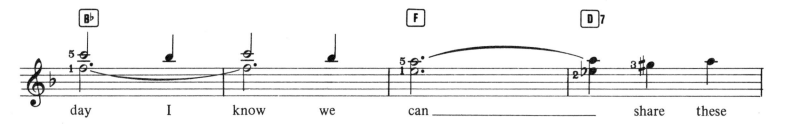

day   I   know   we   can _____ share   these

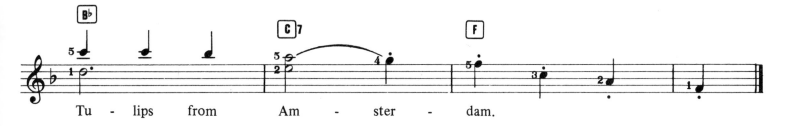

Tu - lips   from   Am - ster - dam.

SIXTEENTH NOTES (SEMIQUAVERS), AND DOTTED RHYTHMS

An eighth note (quaver) can be subdivided into two sixteenth notes (semiquavers):-

eighth note   sixteenth notes

A dotted eighth note is equal to half as much again (see "dotted time notes", Book Two, p. 75), that is, three sixteenth notes:-

dotted eighth note   sixteenth notes

In practice a dotted eighth note usually pairs up with a sixteenth note:-

dotted eighth note   sixteenth note

Together, these two time notes are equivalent to 4 sixteenth notes, or 1 quarter note (crotchet):-

3 sixteenth notes + 1 sixteenth note = quarter note

The general effect of a passage like:-

is of eighth notes (quavers) with a "lilt".

The phrase "humpty dumpty" is a useful guide to this rhythm:-

say: Hump-ty Dump-ty Hump-ty Dump-ty

▲   ▲   ▲   ▲
stress   stress   stress   stress

These uneven types of rhythms are often called Dotted Rhythms.
Look out for dotted rhythms in the next four pieces.

SCALE OF G; KEY OF G

7

Scale of G (major)

G   A   B   C   D   E   (F♯)   G

An F Sharp is required to form the scale of G. When a piece is built on this scale it is said to be in the "key of G". When you are playing in this key you must remember to play all F's, wherever they might fall on the keyboard, as F Sharps. The key signature, which appears at the beginning of every line, will remind you:-

key of G

key signature

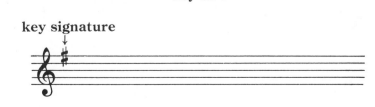

YELLOW SUBMARINE

Words & Music by John Lennon & Paul McCartney

Suggested registration: piano

Rhythm: swing
Tempo: medium (♩ = 100)
Synchro-start, if available

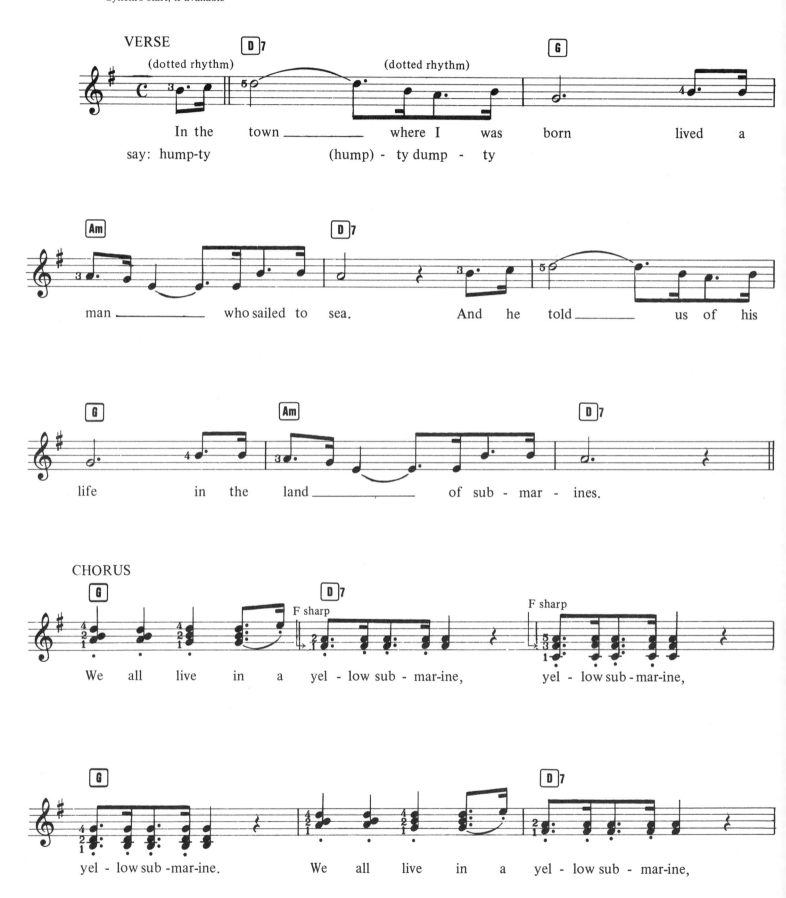

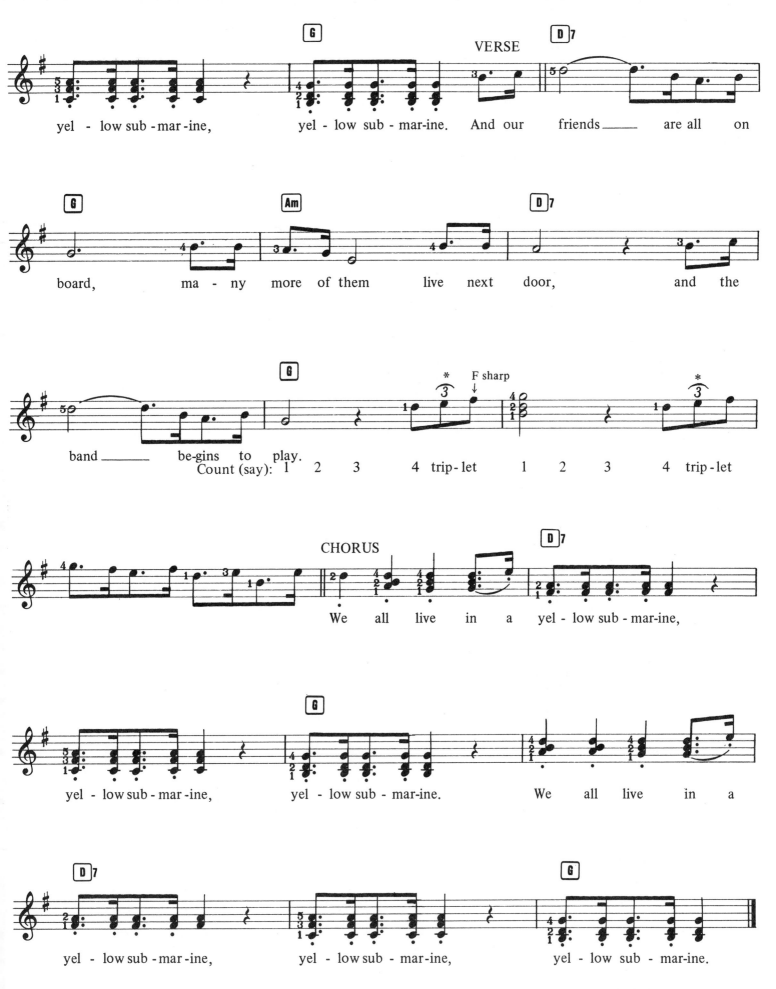

*Triplet. A triplet is a group of 3 notes played in the time of 2. These three eighth notes (quavers) must be played slightly faster than normal eighth notes, in order to fit them into the bar.

CHORD OF B7

8

Using single-finger chord method:

Locate "B" in the accompaniment section of your keyboard. Convert this into "B7" (see Book One, p. 42ff., and your owner's manual).

(see Book One, p. 42ff.

Using fingered chord method:

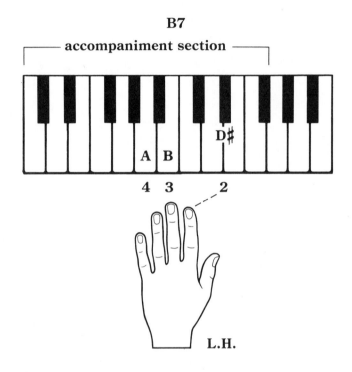

B7

CHANSON D'AMOUR

Words & Music by Wayne Shanklin

Suggested registration: clarinet

Rhythm: swing
Tempo: medium (♩ = 100)

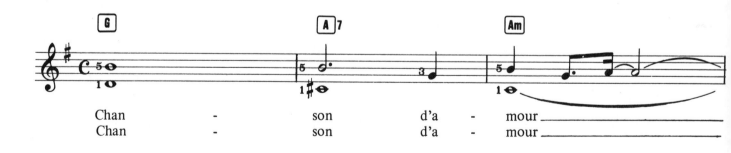

Chan - son d'a - mour _____
Chan - son d'a - mour _____

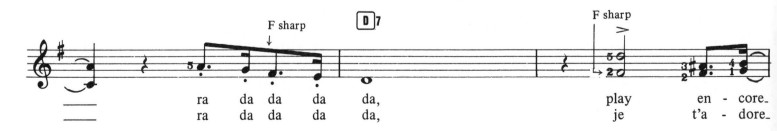

_____ ra da da da da,   play   en - core
_____ ra da da da da,   je   t'a - dore

117

WHEN I'M SIXTY-FOUR

Words & Music by John Lennon & Paul McCartney

Suggested registration: funny +
duet (if available)

Rhythm: swing
Tempo: medium (♩ = 108)
Synchro-start, if available

When I get old - er, los - ing my hair __ ma - ny __ years from

now, will you still be send - ing me a Val - en - tine __

birth - day greet - ings, bot - tle of wine? __ If I'd been out __ till

quar - ter to three __ would you lock the door?

Will you still need __ me, will you still feed __ me, when I'm six - ty __

Change funny to flute
FINE

four?

Ev - 'ry sum - mer we can rent a cot - tage in the Isle of

Wight, if it's not too dear. We shall

F sharp

scrimp and save

Ah grand - child - ren on your knee

Ve - ra, Chuck, and

(N.C.)   ↓ flute to funny

D.C. al FINE

↑ stop rhythm (with L.H.) *

Dave.

*leave synchro button on, and rhythm will start again automatically when you strike the next chord ("G", at the beginning of the piece).

CHORDS OF G MINOR (Gm), AND B♭ MINOR (B♭m)

Using single-finger chord method:

Locate "G" and "B♭" in the accompaniment section of your keyboard. Convert these notes into "Gm" and "B♭m"

respectively (see Book Two, p. 74, and your owner's manual).

Using fingered chord method:

Gm

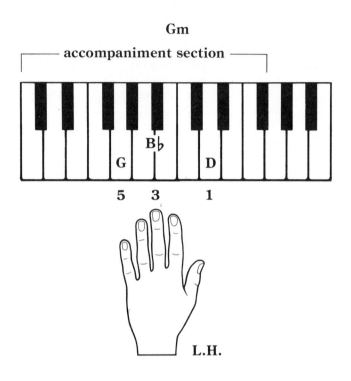

Compare this chord to G (major), a chord you already know.

B♭m

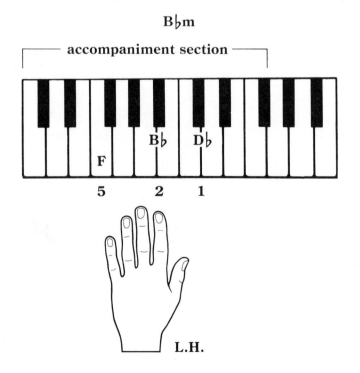

Compare this chord to Bb (major), a chord you already know.

ISN'T SHE LOVELY

Words & Music by Stevie Wonder

Suggested registration: piano +
sustain

Rhythm: swing
Tempo: medium (♩ = 112)
Synchro-start, if available

Is - n't she love - ly_____ Is - n't she won - der - ful? ____

___ Is - n't she pre - cious_____ less than one

min - ute old?_____ I nev - er thought___ through love we'd

be mak - ing one as love - ly as she. Is - n't she

D.C. (Repeat and Fade)

love - ly, made from love. ___ Stop rhythm (with L.H.)

*Quarter Note (Crotchet) Triplet. 3
quarter notes played in the time of 2.
Play these quarter notes slightly faster

than usual, in order to fit them into the
bar, but keep them even, and equal to
each other.

DREAM LOVER

Words by Clifford Grey
Music by Victor Schertzinger

Suggested registration: violin
solo

Rhythm: waltz
Tempo: medium (♩ = 84)

*Acciaccatura. A purely ornamental note,
not included in the timing of the bar. Play
the acciaccatura note as quickly as
possible.

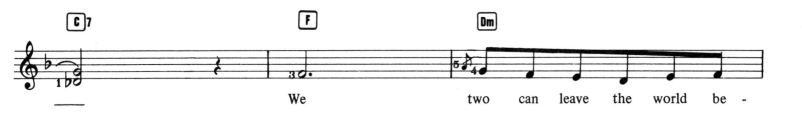

We

two can leave the world be-

hind

us.

No -

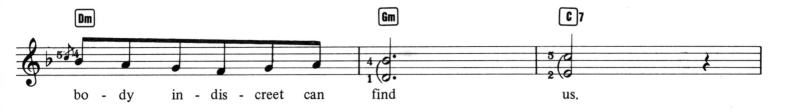

bo - dy in - dis - creet can find

us.

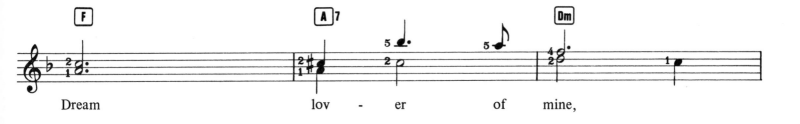

Dream

lov - er of mine,

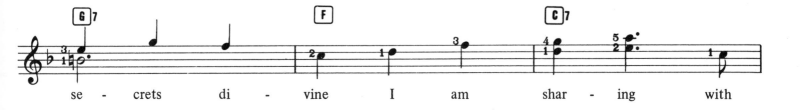

se - crets di - vine I am shar - ing with

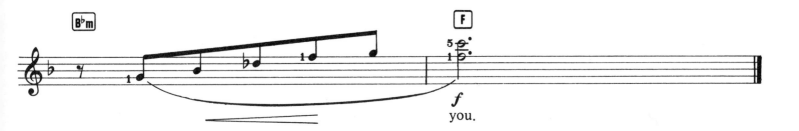

you.

MINOR KEYS

10
So far almost all your playing has been in major keys: C, F, and G. Songs written in minor keys, with their preponderance of minor chords, often have a sad, nostalgic quality, which makes an excellent contrast.

KEY OF D MINOR

11
The key of D Minor is related to the key of F Major. The scales on which these keys are built use the same notes:

scale of D Minor

scale of F

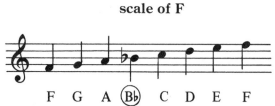

All the notes are white except one: B Flat. As you would expect, both keys have the same key signature:

key of D Minor

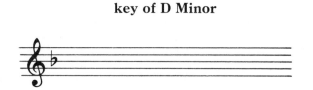

key of F

When playing in the key of D Minor (as in the key of F), you must remember to play all B's, wherever they might fall on the keyboard, as B Flats.

SUNNY

Words & Music by Bobby Hebb

Suggested registration: *jazz organ,*
with stereo chorus.

Rhythm: *rock*
Tempo: *medium (♩ = 96)*

Sun - ny yes - ter - day my life was filled with rain. Sun - ny you smiled at me and real - ly eased the pain, oh the dark days are done and the bright days are here, my Sun - ny one shines so sin - cere, oh, Sun - ny one so true, I love you.

HAVA NAGILA

Traditional

Suggested registration: clarinet
Rhythm: march $\frac{2}{4}$ (or swing)
Tempo: medium (♩ = 88)

* Grace Notes. Purely ornamental notes
  not included in the basic timing of the
  bar. Play your grace notes as quickly as
  possible.

Change clarinet to
harpsichord 2nd time

Add arpeggio

(Speed up tempo control, bit by bit, with left hand)

(leave tempo control now)

Stop rhythm

KEY OF E MINOR

12 The key of E Minor is related to the key of G Major. Both keys use the same scale notes:

scale of E Minor

scale of G

All the notes are white except one: F Sharp.

The key signature is the same for both keys:

key of E Minor

key of G

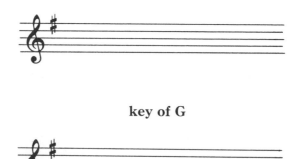

When playing in the key of E Minor (as in the key of G), you must remember to play all F's, wherever they might fall on the keyboard, as F Sharps.

TABOO

Words by S. K. Russell
Spanish words & music by Margarita Lecuona

Suggested registration: clarinet

Rhythm: tango
Tempo: medium (♩ = 116)

ANNIVERSARY SONG

Words & Music by Al Jolson & Saul Chaplin

Suggested registration: violin

Rhythm: waltz
Tempo: quite fast (♩ = 160)

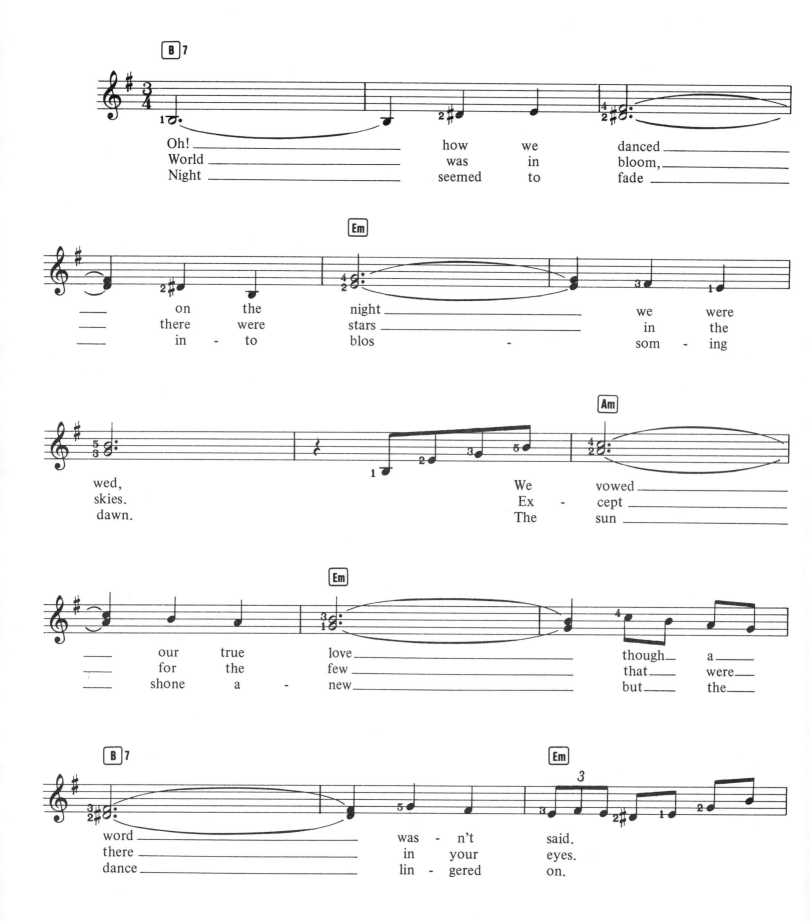

KEY OF B FLAT

13 The scale of B Flat, and therefore the key of B Flat, requires two flats: B Flat, and E Flat:—

scale/key of B Flat (major)

key signature

B♭   C   D   E♭   F   G   A   B♭

When you are playing in this key you must remember to play all B's and E's, wherever they might fall on the keyboard, as B Flats and E Flats, respectively.

CHORD OF E♭ (MAJOR)

14 Using single-finger chord method:

Play the note "E♭" (the higher one of two) in the accompaniment section of your keyboard.

Using fingered chord method:

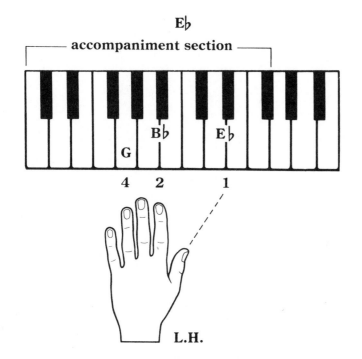

DON'T CRY FOR ME ARGENTINA

Music by Andrew Lloyd Webber
Lyrics by Tim Rice

Suggested registration: Trumpet

Rhythm: tango
Tempo: medium (♩ = 112)

MAMMA MIA

Words & Music by Benny Andersson, Stig Anderson & Bjorn Ulvaeus

Suggested registration: synth. guitar

Rhythm: rock
Tempo: medium (♩ = 126)

I've been cheat-ed by you____ since I don't know when.
So I made up my mind____ it must come to an end.

Look at me now____ will I ev-er learn?

I don't know how____ but I sud-den-ly lose____ con-trol

There's a fire ____ with-in my soul _____ just a

look and I can hear a bell ring____ One more look and I for-get ev-'ry-thing__

CHORUS

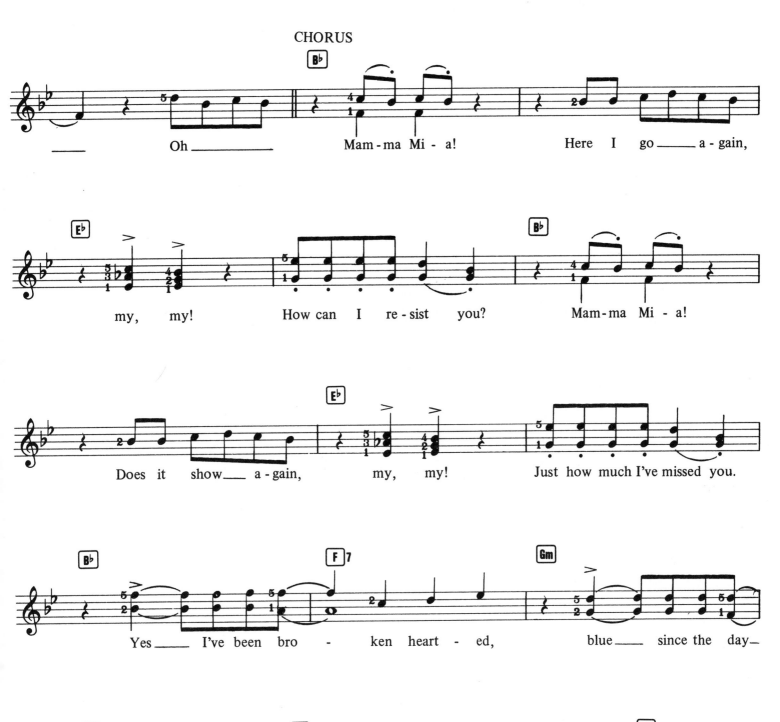

Oh _____ Mam-ma Mi - a! Here I go _____ a-gain, my, my! How can I re-sist you? Mam-ma Mi - a! Does it show _____ a-gain, my, my! Just how much I've missed you.

Yes _____ I've been bro - ken heart - ed, blue _____ since the day _____ we part - ed, why, why, did I ev-er let _____ you

go?

CHORD OF C MINOR (Cm)

15

Using single-finger chord method:

Locate "C" (the higher one of two) in the accompaniment section of your keyboard. Convert this note into "Cm" (see Book Two, p. 74, and your owner's manual).

Using fingered chord method:

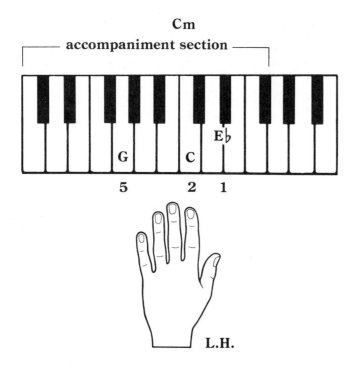

Compare this chord to C (major), a chord you already know.

RAINDROPS KEEP FALLING ON MY HEAD

Words by Hal David
Music by Burt Bacharach

Suggested registration: electric guitar

Rhythm: Swing
Tempo: medium (♩ = 104)

Rain - drops keep fall - in' on my head,
did me some talk - in' to the sun.

To Coda ⊕

just like the guy whose feet are too big for his bed, no - thing seems to
I said I did - n't like the way he got things done, sleep - in' on the

fit, those rain - drops are fall - in' on my head, they keep fall - in', ___
job, those rain - drops are fall - in' on my head, they keep fall - in', ___

So I just
But there's one thing I know, the

blues they send to meet me won't de - feat me, it

won't be long ___ till hap - pi - ness steps up to greet ___ me.

D.C. al Coda

⊕ *CODA*

Be - cause I'm

free _____ no-thin's wor-ry-ing me. _____

TELSTAR

By Joe Meek

Suggested registration: jazz organ,
with tremolo

Rhythm: disco
Tempo: medium (♩ = 120)

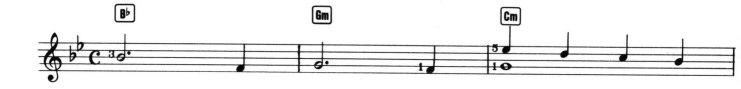

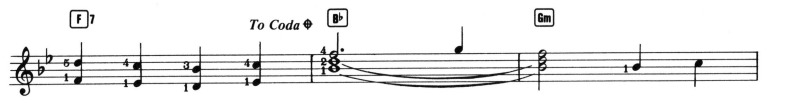

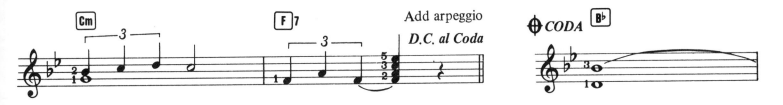

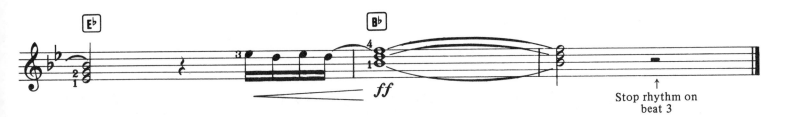

CHORD CHART (Showing all "fingered chords" used in the course)

16

C
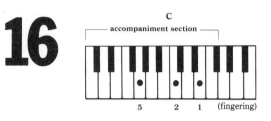
accompaniment section
5   2   1   (fingering)

Cm
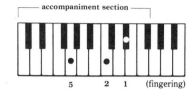
accompaniment section
5   2   1   (fingering)

C7
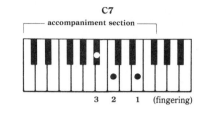
accompaniment section
3   2   1   (fingering)

Dm
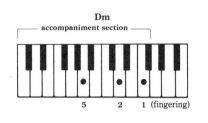
accompaniment section
5   2   1 (fingering)

D7
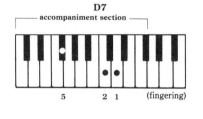
accompaniment section
5   2   1   (fingering)

E♭
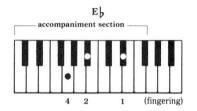
accompaniment section
4   2   1   (fingering)

Em
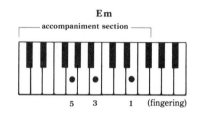
accompaniment section
5   3   1   (fingering)

E7
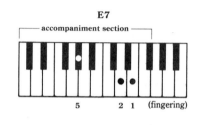
accompaniment section
5   2   1   (fingering)

F
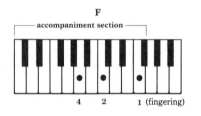
accompaniment section
4   2   1   (fingering)

Fm
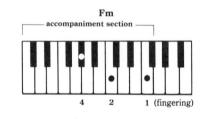
accompaniment section
4   2   1   (fingering)

F7
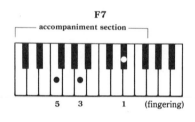
accompaniment section
5   3   1   (fingering)

G
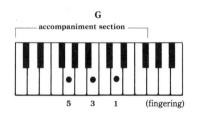
accompaniment section
5   3   1   (fingering)

Gm
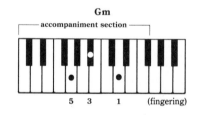
accompaniment section
5   3   1   (fingering)

G7
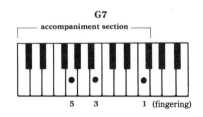
accompaniment section
5   3   1   (fingering)

Am
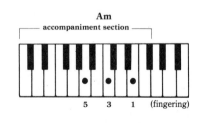
accompaniment section
5   3   1   (fingering)

A7
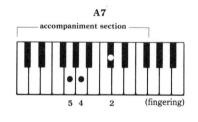
accompaniment section
5 4   2   (fingering)

B♭
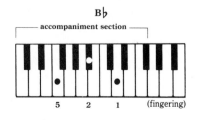
accompaniment section
5   2   1   (fingering)

B♭m
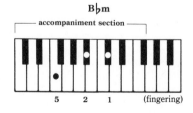
accompaniment section
5   2   1   (fingering)

B7
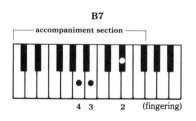
accompaniment section
4   3   2   (fingering)

Checklist of important piano books.
The books below are available from your local music shop who will order them for you if not in stock.
If there is no music shop near you, you may order direct from Music Sales Limited (Dept. M), 8/9 Frith Street, London W1V 5TZ.
Please always include £1 to cover post/packing costs.

A Start At The Piano
AM 40650

Alison Bell's Graded For Piano Pieces Book 1: Very Easy
AM 30297

Book 5: Upper Intermediate
AM 30339

Anthology Of Piano Music Volume 1: Baroque
AM 10968

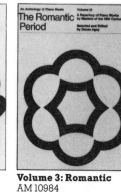
Volume 3: Romantic
AM 10984

Barrelhouse And Boogie Piano
OK 64659

Big Note Piano Book 1
AM 28226

Bud Powell: Jazz Masters Series
AM 23219

Chord Guide To Pop Music
AM 10596

The Classic Piano Repertoire Bach
EW 50023

Chopin
EW 50015

Promenade Theory Papers Book 1
PB 40583

Classics To Moderns Book 1
YK 20014

Classics To Moderns Sonatas & Sonatinas
YK 20204

Themes & Variations
YK 20196

More Classics To Moderns Book 1
YK 20121

Dave Brubeck: Jazz Masters Series
AM 21189

Easy Classical Piano Duets
AM 31949

The Complete Piano Player By Kenneth Baker Book 1
AM 34828

Book 2
AM 34836

Book 3
AM 34844

Book 4
AM 34851

Book 5
AM 34869

Style Book
AM 35338

Improvising Rock Piano
AM 22039

Easy Piano Solos
Simple Arrangements
of Pop Classics
AM 28648

**For Your Eyes Only & 18
Movie Themes**
AM 36609

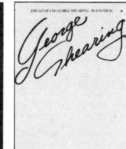

**Genius Of George
Shearing**
AM 25990

Genius Of Art Tatum
BG 10085

Genius Of Fats Waller
AM 24423

Genius of Andre Previn
AM 25982

**Genius Of Jazz Giants
Volume 1**
AM 36708

Jazz Hanon
AM 27418

Blues Hanon
AM 27889

Boogie Woogie Hanon
AM 27400

**Home Piano Library
Classics**
AM 34141

Rock 'n' Roll
AM 36922

Showmusic
AM 36724

Hooked On Classics
AM 32210

How To Play Blues Piano
AM 35197

**How To Play Boogie-
Woogie**
AM 33317

Improvising Rock Piano
AM 22039

Ballet Music
AM 32939

Beatles
NO 17907

Rock and Roll
AM 19556

Elvis
AM 20868

Familiar Songs
AM 36419

Paul Simon
PS 10214

Christmas Songs
AM 22641

Walt Disney
WD 10260

Jazz Riffs For Piano
AM 21502

**The Joy Of
Bach**
YK 21004

Boogie and Blues
YK 21020

Christmas
YK 21194

Folk Songs
YK 21061

Mozart
YK 21244

Piano Entertainment
YK 21178

Romantic Piano: Book 1
YJK 21145

First Year Piano
YK 21053

Piano Duets
YK 21111

Pianist's Picture Chords
AM 21429

The Piano Chord Finder
AM 24860

More Piano Pieces For Children
YK 20220

The Music Of Michel Legrand
AM 25727

Piano Adventures Pop Blends
AM 32079

I Love Pop
AM 32087

Popular Piano Solos Book 1
AM 24100

Book 7: Blues
AM 33879

Book 8: Jazz
AM 33861

Easy Classical Piano Duets
AM 31949

Easy Folk Piano Duets
AM 31956

Ragtime: 100 Authentic Rags
AM 25081

Rock Keyboard Styles
(with cassette)
DG 20017

The Best Of McCartney Easy Piano
MY 70101

Songs Of World War II
AM 14226

Teach Yourself Rock Piano
AM 25172

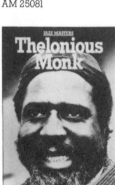

Teaching Piano (Combined) By Denes Agay.
YK 20279

Thelonious Monk: Jazz Masters Series
AM 19423

They All Played Ragtime
OK 61572

Timeless Standards
AM 36641

Timeless Country Standards
AM 36658

Timeless Jazz Standards
AM 36666

Tomorrow: 18 Broadway Blockbusters
AM 36617

With My Love
AM 25925

1/90